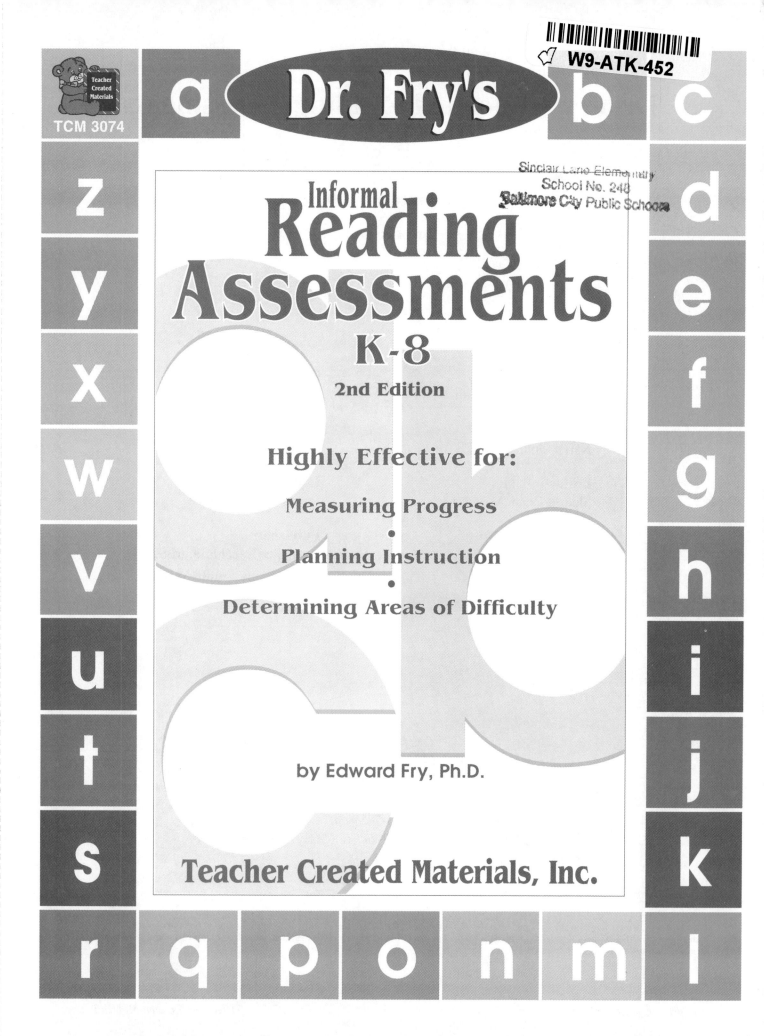

Dr. Fry's

Informal
Reading
Assessments
K-8
2nd Edition

Highly Effective for:

Measuring Progress

·

Planning Instruction

·

Determining Areas of Difficulty

by Edward Fry, Ph.D.

Teacher Created Materials, Inc.

Dr. Fry's Informal Reading Assessments

K–8

by Edward Fry, Ph.D.

2nd Edition

Editor
Lori Grodin, M.S. Ed.

Editorial Manager
Karen Goldfluss, M.S. Ed.

Editor-in-Chief
Sharon Coan, M.S. Ed.

Art Coordinator
Denice Adorno

Illustrator
Ken Tunell

Cover Artist
Jamie Sochin

Product Manager
Phil Garcia

Imaging
James Edward Grace

Publishers
Rachelle Cracchiolo, M.S. Ed.

Mary Dupuy Smith, M.S. Ed.

Teacher Created Materials, Inc.
6421 Industry Way
Westminster, CA 92683
www.teachercreated.com
ISBN-0-7439-3074-6
©2001 Teacher Created Materials, Inc.
Reprinted, 2004
Made in U.S.A.

Table of Contents

*Numbers in parentheses are approximate reading ability grade levels.

Introduction

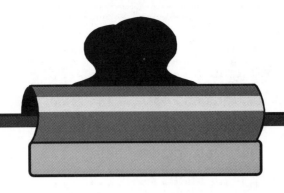

These tests are intended to help teachers of reading by determining what should be taught, measuring progress, and suggesting areas that might be causing difficulty in learning to read.

They are useful for elementary teachers, parents, remedial or special education teachers, reading teachers, volunteer tutors, adult literacy teachers, and teachers of students learning English.

It is not suggested that you need to use all of the tests provided; choose the ones most appropriate to assess the needs of your students.

Many of the enclosed assessments include teaching suggestions. These ideas and the references and materials used at the back of the book are not exhaustive but offer an assortment of strategies to use as needed.

Your efforts in teaching someone to read are worthwhile and commendable.

Edward Fry, Ph.D.

Oral Reading Test

Purpose

This test quickly determines a student's general reading level.

Answer Key

Mark the examiner's copy and record sheet.

Count one mistake for each word the student is unable to pronounce. If the student immediately makes the correction, this is not counted as a mistake. If a student omits a word, ask the student to read the line again more carefully.

Underline each word the student can't pronounce or needs help in pronouncing. When the student has finished reading a paragraph, count the mistakes and check the appropriate box to the right of each paragraph. For example, if a student begins with paragraph 1-B and reads it without a mistake, or with one or two mistakes, she/he can read at this level independently. Check "Indep." to the right of the paragraph.

The student should then read paragraph 2-A. If the student receives a score of 0–2 mistakes, then the student can handle material at this level independently, too. Check "Indep." The student next reads paragraph 2-B. If she/he makes three to four mistakes, you have found the instructional reading level. Check "Instr." to the right of that paragraph. This is the level at which reading instruction will be most effective for that student. Notice that the number of mistakes for each reading level is shown on the test to the right of the paragraph.

After finding the student's instructional reading level, continue the test until you find the frustration reading level. Check "Frust." to the right of the paragraph. Stop testing when you get to the student's frustration level.

Record the results of the test in the spaces provided on the examiner's copy of the test. Fill in the highest grade level of material that the student can handle independently. Then record the grade level of material that should be used for instruction.

Oral Reading Test *(cont.)*

Do not use this test for instruction. If a student misses a word, tell that student to "go on." Do not supply any hints or tell the student the word. If this policy is followed, the same test can be used later to determine progress. When retesting a student, use different colored pencils to underline mistakes. Spaces have been provided for recording the results of the retests. Keep the record sheet for easy reference and for retesting.

The paragraphs are not timed, but excessive rapidity or slowness may be noted to the right of the paragraph as a characteristic of the student's reading ability. Slow reading means more practice is needed at that level so the student can gain fluency.

There are two paragraphs per grade level for grades one through three. The first paragraph is marked 1-A. This means "easy first grade." The next is marked 1-B. This means "hard first grade." There is only one paragraph for each level beyond third.

The last paragraph is marked grade seven, but actually it is indicative of popular adult and non-academic reading or a non-technical secondary reading level. If a student can read it without errors, she or he can do most junior and senior high school reading satisfactorily. For more accurate determination of reading ability for students reading at junior and senior high school levels, a standardized silent reading test is recommended. *If the last paragraph is read at the Independent Level, use a silent reading test to determine advanced skills.*

Teaching Suggestions

1. To improve general reading ability, see the book *How to Teach Reading*, which includes many strategies such as easy reading practice, comprehension instruction, phonics, vocabulary improvement, and development of writing skills.

2. Oral reading can be improved by practicing reading aloud from material at the student's independent or instructional level. See the readability graph on page 79 for determining book difficulty.

3. Use a variety of oral reading experiences such as reading short passages, poems, parts in plays, and announcements.

Oral Reading Test

Examiner's Copy and Record Sheet
for Determining Independent and Instructional Reading Levels

Student's Name _____ Date_____

Examiner_____ Class _____

	1st Testing	2nd Testing	3rd Testing
Date	_____	_____	_____
Total Score: Independent reading level	_____	_____	_____
	Grade	Grade	Grade
Instructional reading level	_____	_____	_____
	Grade	Grade	Grade

Directions: The student reads aloud from the student copy—not this copy. If the student can't read a word or mispronounces it, just say "Go on," and count it as an error (underline the word). Do not tell the student the missed word. Stop the test when the Frustration Level is first reached.

No. 1-A (Easy First Grade)	Errors	Level	1st Testing	2nd Testing	3rd Testing
Look at the dog.	0–2	Indep.	☐	☐	☐
	3–4	Instr.	☐	☐	☐
It is big.	5+	Frust.	☐	☐	☐
It can run.	Speed:	Fast	☐	☐	☐
		Avg.	☐	☐	☐
Run, dog, run away.		Slow	☐	☐	☐
		Very slow	☐	☐	☐

No. 1-B (Hard First Grade)	Errors	Level	1st Testing	2nd Testing	3rd Testing
We saw the sun.	0–2	Indep.	☐	☐	☐
	3–4	Instr.	☐	☐	☐
It made us warm.	5+	Frust.	☐	☐	☐
Now it was time to go home.	Speed:	Fast	☐	☐	☐
		Avg.	☐	☐	☐
It was a long way to walk.		Slow	☐	☐	☐
		Very slow	☐	☐	☐

Oral Reading Test *(cont.)*

			1st Testing	2nd Testing	3rd Testing
No. 2-A (Easy Second Grade)	**Errors**	**Level**			
	0–2	Indep.	☐	☐	☐
The door of the house opened, and a	3–4	Instr.	☐	☐	☐
man came out. He had a broom in his	5+	Frust.	☐	☐	☐
hand. He said to the boy sitting there,					
"Go away." The boy got up and left.	Speed:	Fast	☐	☐	☐
		Avg.	☐	☐	☐
		Slow	☐	☐	☐
		Very slow	☐	☐	☐

			1st Testing	2nd Testing	3rd Testing
No. 2-B (Hard Second Grade)	**Errors**	**Level**			
	0–2	Indep.	☐	☐	☐
The family ate breakfast. Then they gave	3–4	Instr.	☐	☐	☐
the pig his breakfast. It was fun to watch	5+	Frust.	☐	☐	☐
him eat. He seemed to like it. He was					
eating all of it.	Speed:	Fast	☐	☐	☐
		Avg.	☐	☐	☐
		Slow	☐	☐	☐
		Very slow	☐	☐	☐

			1st Testing	2nd Testing	3rd Testing
No. 3-A (Easy Third Grade)	**Errors**	**Level**			
	0–2	Indep.	☐	☐	☐
When the man had gone, the boys were	3–4	Instr.	☐	☐	☐
surprised to see how many boxes he had left	5+	Frust.	☐	☐	☐
in their little backyard. Right away they					
began to pile them on top of each other. It	Speed:	Fast	☐	☐	☐
took so long that lunchtime came before		Avg.	☐	☐	☐
they knew they were hungry.		Slow	☐	☐	☐
		Very slow	☐	☐	☐

			1st Testing	2nd Testing	3rd Testing
No. 3-B (Hard Third Grade)	**Errors**	**Level**			
	0–2	Indep.	☐	☐	☐
The man became angry because his dog	3–4	Instr.	☐	☐	☐
had never talked before, and besides, he	5+	Frust.	☐	☐	☐
didn't like its voice. So he took his knife					
and cut a branch from a palm tree. Just	Speed:	Fast	☐	☐	☐
then the palm tree said, "Put down that		Avg.	☐	☐	☐
branch." The man was getting very upset		Slow	☐	☐	☐
about the way things were going, and he		Very slow	☐	☐	☐
started to throw the branch away.					

Oral Reading Test *(cont.)*

No. 4 (Fourth Grade)

Three more cowboys tried their best to rope and tie a calf as quickly as Red, but none of them came within ten seconds of his time. Then came the tall, thin cowboy. He was the last one to enter the contest.

Errors	Level	1st Testing	2nd Testing	3rd Testing
0–2	Indep.	☐	☐	☐
3–4	Instr.	☐	☐	☐
5+	Frust.	☐	☐	☐
Speed:	Fast	☐	☐	☐
	Avg.	☐	☐	☐
	Slow	☐	☐	☐
	Very slow	☐	☐	☐

No. 5 (Fifth Grade)

High in the hills they came to a wide ledge where trees grew among the rocks. Grass grew in patches, and the ground was covered with bits of wood from trees blown over a long time ago and dried by the sun. Down in the valley it was already beginning to get dark.

Errors	Level	1st Testing	2nd Testing	3rd Testing
0–2	Indep.	☐	☐	☐
3–4	Instr.	☐	☐	☐
5+	Frust.	☐	☐	☐
Speed:	Fast	☐	☐	☐
	Avg.	☐	☐	☐
	Slow	☐	☐	☐
	Very slow	☐	☐	☐

No. 6 (Sixth Grade)

Businessmen from suburban areas may travel to work in helicopters, land on the roof of an office building, and thus avoid city traffic jams. Families can spend more time at summer homes and mountain cabins through the use of this marvelous craft. People on farms can reach city centers quickly for medical service, shopping, entertainment, or sale of products.

Errors	Level	1st Testing	2nd Testing	3rd Testing
0–2	Indep.	☐	☐	☐
3–4	Instr.	☐	☐	☐
5+	Frust.	☐	☐	☐
Speed:	Fast	☐	☐	☐
	Avg.	☐	☐	☐
	Slow	☐	☐	☐
	Very slow	☐	☐	☐

No. 7 (Seventh Grade)

The president of the United States was speaking. His audience was comprised of two thousand foreign-born men who had just been admitted to citizenship. They listened intently, their faces aglow with the light of a newborn patriotism, upturned to the calm, intellectual face of the first citizen of the country they now claimed as their own.

Errors	Level	1st Testing	2nd Testing	3rd Testing
0–2	Indep.	☐	☐	☐
3–4	Instr.	☐	☐	☐
5+	Frust.	☐	☐	☐
Speed:	Fast	☐	☐	☐
	Avg.	☐	☐	☐
	Slow	☐	☐	☐
	Very slow	☐	☐	☐

Oral Reading Test

Name: _____

Directions: Read aloud from this copy. The teacher marks errors on the Examiner's Copy, pages 7, 8, 9.

No. 1-A

Look at the dog.

It is big.

It can run.

Run, dog, run away.

No. 1-B

We saw the sun.

It made us warm.

Now it was time to go home.

It was a long way to walk.

No. 2-A

The door of the house opened, and a man came out.

He had a broom in his hand. He said to the boy sitting there, "Go away."

The boy got up and left.

No. 2-B

The family ate breakfast. Then they gave the pig his breakfast. It was fun to watch him eat. He seemed to like it. He was eating all of it.

No. 3-A

When the man had gone, the boys were surprised to see how many boxes he had left in their little backyard. Right away they began to pile them on top of each other. It took so long that lunchtime came before they knew they were hungry.

Oral Reading Test *(cont.)*

No. 3-B

The man became angry because his dog had never talked before, and besides, he didn't like its voice. So he took his knife and cut a branch from a palm tree. Just then the palm tree said, "Put down that branch." The man was getting very upset about the way things were going, and he started to throw the branch away.

No. 4

Three more cowboys tried their best to rope and tie a calf as quickly as Red, but none of them came within ten seconds of his time. Then came the tall, thin cowboy. He was the last one to enter the contest.

No. 5

High in the hills they came to a wide ledge where trees grew among the rocks. Grass grew in patches, and the ground was covered with bits of wood from trees blown over a long time ago and dried by the sun. Down in the valley it was already beginning to get dark.

No. 6

Businessmen from suburban areas may travel to work in helicopters, land on the roof of an office building, and thus avoid city traffic jams. Families can spend more time at summer homes and mountain cabins through the use of this marvelous craft. People on farms can reach city centers quickly for medical service, shopping, entertainment, or sale of products.

No. 7

The president of the United States was speaking. His audience was comprised of two thousand foreign-born men who had just been admitted to citizenship. They listened intently, their faces aglow with the light of a newborn patriotism, upturned to the calm, intellectual face of the first citizen of the country they now claimed as their own.

Phonics Survey Test

Purpose

The purpose is to quickly assess a student's phonics skills through oral reading of nonsense words.

This test is designed to give you a rough idea of your student's total phonics (decoding) ability in just a few minutes. The test is partly diagnostic in that it gives you an idea of the student's competence in six areas: easy consonants, short vowels, hard consonants, long vowels, consonant digraphs, and difficult vowels.

Administration and Scoring

Ask the student to read the nonsense words aloud from the Phonics Survey Test. Tell the student that these are not real words. If the student makes an error, allow a second chance (but not a third).

Use the examiner's copy to mark each letter the student reads incorrectly. Then check the appropriate box to summarize the student's performance. This information will be useful in selecting materials for reading instruction.

Be careful in marking your examiner's copy and listen carefully. A student might pronounce the consonant sound of a nonsense word correctly and the vowel sound incorrectly. This test is a little tricky to score correctly, so take your time and remember it only yields a rough approximation of a student's skills.

Phonics is an important and useful skill associated with reading. Poor ability in phonics does not always mean poor reading ability, but if a student's reading ability is poor, it can often be aided by having the student's reading instruction include phonics lessons.

Do not do the whole test if the student is weak in the first section.

Suggested Student Reading Ability Level: Grades 1–4

Teaching Suggestions

1. Pause during oral reading and help the student sound out the beginning of an unknown word.
2. Systematically teach some or most phonics (phoneme grapheme correspondence) using phonics charts.
3. Use flashcards, one for each phoneme grapheme correspondence (letter sound relationship).
4. Use phonics workbooks or drill sheets.
5. Teach phonics as part of a spelling lesson.
6. Teach phonics as part of dictionary use.
7. Teach phonograms.

Phonics Survey Test

Examiner's Copy

Name: _____

> **Total Number of Words Correct:** _____
> **Number Possible: 18**

Directions: Have the student read aloud each nonsense word from the student test page. Mark each letter or letters the student reads incorrectly. Then check the appropriate box to summarize the student's performance.

					Knew All	Knew Some	Knew None
Section 1	TIF	NEL	ROM	Easy Consonants	☐	☐	☐
	DUP	CAV	SEB	Short Vowels	☐	☐	☐
Section 2	KO	HOAB	WAJE	Hard Consonants	☐	☐	☐
	ZEEX	QUIDE	YAIG	Long Vowels	☐	☐	☐
Section 3	WHAW	THOIM	PHER	Consonant Digraphs	☐	☐	☐
	OUSH	CHAU	EANG	Difficult Vowels	☐	☐	☐

Name _____

Phonics Survey Test

Directions: Read the nonsense words aloud. The examiner marks the examiner's copy.

Section 1	TIF	NEL	ROM
	DUP	CAV	SEB
Section 2	KO	HOAB	WAJE
	ZEEX	QUIDE	YAIG
Section 3	WHAW	THOIM	PHER
	OUSH	CHAU	EANG

Phonics Patterns Test

Purpose

This will help the teacher quickly find the level of phonics pattern development of any student, child or adult.

Administration and Scoring

Make a copy of the test on the next page for the student. Simply ask the student to read the nonsense words in each category. Note on a separate sheet of paper or a copy of this test where errors are made. There is an easy (or common) rime, or a harder (less common) rime in each nonsense word. If the student recognizes or knows the onset and the rime (vowel plus final consonant), she/he should be able to sound out each nonsense word.

It is not necessary to do the whole test in one sitting. Test a few categories, rest, teach to discovered needs, and test more categories later.

Some vowel spellings can have more than one sound. For example, "EA" is a Long A in "great" and a Long E in "seat." Try to get the student to use the sound you are testing. As you teach these phonogram families, these different spellings (letters) for the same vowel sound will become readily apparent.

Suggested Reading Ability Level: Grades 2–5

Teaching Suggestions

1. Show as many example words that illustrate one rime family as possible. For example, "ball, call, fall, hall," etc.

2. Have a spelling test of just two families or rimes.

3. Make cards with onsets (consonants) on one card and rimes on another set of cards. Student matches them to make words.

4. Make word wheels or slip charts that substitute different onsets in front of rimes.

Name _____

Phonics Patterns Test

Directions: The student reads the nonsense words aloud. The examiner marks errors on a separate copy.

	Easy Patterns	**Harder Patterns**
Short A Sound	mab fam	thasp sance
Long A Sound	jace baint	shaze crange
Broad A Sound	dar mard	tharge narp
Short E Sound	jed ket	threlp betch
Long E Sound	ree geat	smief scheave
Short I Sound	pib glig	stisp trinch
Long I Sound	pice kile	drize phie
Short O Sound	pob bot	swomp trox
Long O Sound	moe goke	skown flost
Short OO Sound	dook tood	brould froor
Long OO Sound	poot mue	thew floup

Name _____

Phonics Patterns Test *(cont.)*

	Easy Patterns	**Harder Patterns**
Broad O	nall lork	choar quawl
OI Sound	noil croy	wroist foin
OU Sound	jour fout	shouse kounce
Short U	pum grunk	lutch sudge
UR Sound	hern surn	zirl slurse

Onset and Rime Test

Purpose

This test is an alternate test to the Phonics Patterns Test. It tests similar skills in a different way.

Administration and Scoring

Have the student read the nonsense words aloud and record the errors on a separate copy.

There is no correct score; each incorrect item shows a need to teach that onset or that rime.

If the student recognizes or knows the onset (any letter or letters before the vowel) and the rime (vowel plus the final consonant or consonants), he or she should be able to sound out each nonsense word. For example, with the onset test, the student is reading different consonant beginnings for each word, with the endings staying the same, either –up, –and, or –out. For the rime test, the onset is the same in each nonsense word, and the rimes, or endings, change.

Suggested Reading Ability Level: Grades 1–4

Teaching Suggestions

1. Show as many example words that illustrate one rime family as possible. For example, "ball, call, fall, hall," etc.

2. Have a spelling test of just two families or rimes.

3. Make cards with onsets (consonants) on one card and rimes on another set of cards. Student matches them to make words.

4. Make word wheels or slip charts that substitute different onsets in front of rimes.

Footnote: For more information on the z test and up-or-out test see the journal article, "Assessing Decoding from an Onset-Rhyme perspective" by James W. Cunningham, Karen A. Erickson, Stephanie A. Spadorica, David A. Koppenhaver, Patricia M. Cunningham, David E. Yodea, and Michael C. McKenna. *Journal of Literacy Research*, v. 31, No. 4, Dec. 1999.

Name _____

Onset and Rime Test

Directions: The student reads the nonsense words aloud. The examiner marks errors on a separate copy.

Onset Test	
(up-and-out test)	
scup	stup
grup	spup
tup	lup
bup	rup
plup	frup
crup	clup
chup	mup
pand	kand
snand	yand
drand	fland
shand	trand
gand	nand
prand	dand
sland	thand
swout	quout
wout	sout
cout	glout
blout	strout
brout	jout
vout	hout
whout	fout

Rime Test	
(z test)	
zack	zail
zain	zake
zale	zame
zan	zank
zap	zash
zat	zate
zaw	zay
zeat	zell
zest	zice
zick	zide
zight	zill
zin	zine
zing	zink
zip	zit
zock	zoke
zop	zore
zot	zuck
zug	zump
zunk	

Phoneme Segmentation Test

Purpose

This test determines if the student can break a spoken word into individual phonemes.

Teaching Suggestions

Phoneme segmentation is a good predictor of success in learning to read. Students who do well on this learn to be good readers.

Frequently, students who do well on this task already have some reading (phonics) and writing (spelling) skills. But that is not necessary. You can teach phoneme segmentation to most pre-readers just by speaking and having the student listen.

For example: "I am going to say a word and you tell me how many sounds (phonemes) it has."

I say "cat"; you say "/k/ /a/ /t/."

I say "go"; you say "/g/ /ō/."

I say "read"; you say "/r/ /ē/ /d/."

Name _____

Phoneme Segmentation Test

Directions: Do not let the student see the printed test. Provide many opportunities to practice segmenting onset and rimes and segmenting common words. You say the complete word, then say the segmented phonemes like in the examples on page 20. Have the student copy you, saying orally the word and the phonemes. Next have the student try to segment new words with your help.

Practice Words (help the student with these):	
Test Word	Answer
back	/b/ /a/ /k/
black	/b/ /l/ /a/ /k/
pain	/p/ /ā/ /n/
paint	/p/ /ā/ /n/ /t/

Teacher Reads: Test Word	Student Answers:	Teacher Records: Correct	Wrong
1. sale	/s/ /ā/ /l/	_____	_____
2. fire	/f/ /ī/ /r/	_____	_____
3. smile	/s/ /m/ /ī/ /l/	_____	_____
4. cent	/s/ /e/ /n/ /t/	_____	_____
5. get	/g/ /e/ /t/	_____	_____
6. bad	/b/ /a/ /d/	_____	_____
7. band	/b/ /a/ /n/ /d/	_____	_____
8. spit	/s/ /p/ /i/ /t/	_____	_____
9. shot	/sh/ /o/ /t/	_____	_____
10. low	/l/ /ō/	_____	_____
		Total Correct	**Total Wrong**

Instant Word Survey Test

Purpose

This test will quickly determine the approximate number of instant words the student can read (up to the first thousand instant words).

Administration and Scoring

Note that the test should be stopped when the student makes the 5th error (not the 5th consecutive error—simply missing any five words). An error is any failure to say or pronounce the test word correctly.

Do not help the student in any way. Do not tell the student of any error. Simply say, "Try the next word."

To determine the approximate number of instant words known, simply multiply the number of the last correct word by 15.

For example, if the last correct word was 10, then 10 x 15 = 150. Start teaching the instant words with word number 151.

Suggested Reading Ability Level: Grades 1–4

Teaching Suggestions

The instant words are the 3,000 most common words in the English language. The first 100 words make up 50 percent of all written material. The first 300 instant words make up 65 percent of all written material. That is why these words must be recognized instantly for any kind of fluency or comprehension facility.

1. Flashcards: Any word the student does not "instantly" read correctly, set aside for repetition later in the lesson and the next day.

2. Easy Reading: Instant words are encountered in all reading, so encouraging frequent independent reading will increase fluency and word recognition. (Student's independent level on the Oral Reading Test.)

3. Games: Many word games can be created using the instant words. These games are fun and motivating for students to play. Suggested game ideas: Bingo, Pairs, or make a board game.

4. Spelling: Use the instant words for spelling lessons.

Instant Word Survey Test

Directions: The student reads aloud from the student list and the examiner marks this copy. Stop after the student misses any five words. Do not help the student. If the student makes an error or hesitates five seconds, say, "Try the next word."

Student's Name _____

Test for the First 300 Words
(approximately every 15th word in the first 300 words)

1. are	11. why
2. but	12. again
3. which	13. study
4. so	14. last
5. see	15. story
6. now	16. beginning
7. only	17. feet
8. just	18. book
9. too	19. almost
10. small	20. family

Test for the Second 300 Words
(approximately every 15th word in the second 300 words)

21. room	31. bring
22. become	32. check
23. whole	33. heavy
24. toward	34. direction
25. map	35. picked
26. king	36. window
27. certain	37. wide
28. stars	38. sign
29. nothing	39. root
30. stood	40. describe

Instant Word Survey Test *(cont.)*

Test for the Next 400 Words

(approximately every 15th word in the next 400 words)

41. ride	54. provide
42. bed	55. guess
43. lake	56. interesting
44. tiny	57. bell
45. sail	58. chief
46. fight	59. army
47. wrote	60. sharp
48. grew	61. chance
49. save	62. agreed
50. equal	63. dead
51. choose	64. fear
52. direct	65. total
53. flow	66. conditions

Instant Word Survey Test

Directions: Please read this list of words out loud for your teacher.

First Set:

1. are	11. why
2. but	12. again
3. which	13. study
4. so	14. last
5. see	15. story
6. now	16. beginning
7. only	17. feet
8. just	18. book
9. too	19. almost
10. small	20. family

Second Set:

21. room	31. bring
22. become	32. check
23. whole	33. heavy
24. toward	34. direction
25. map	35. picked
26. king	36. window
27. certain	37. wide
28. stars	38. sign
29. nothing	39. root
30. stood	40. describe

Instant Word Survey Test (cont.)

Directions: Please read this list of words out loud for your teacher.

Third Set:

41. ride	54. provide
42. bed	55. guess
43. lake	56. interesting
44. tiny	57. bell
45. sail	58. chief
46. fight	59. army
47. wrote	60. sharp
48. grew	61. chance
49. save	62. agreed
50. equal	63. dead
51. choose	64. fear
52. direct	65. total
53. flow	66. conditions

Instant Word Comprehensive Test

Purpose

This is a test of a student's ability to read every one of the first 300 instant words.

In contrast, the Instant Word Survey Test tests only every 15th word of the first 1,000 instant words. This test is more detailed and is meant to be used with beginning readers to find a more precise starting point for teaching the Instant Words.

Administration and Scoring

The student reads the words aloud. The examiner records correct (**C**) or wrong (**X**) for each word.

Stop the test when the student has made 5 errors and teach the error words.

It takes several years for children who are beginning readers to learn the first 300 instant words.

Suggested Reading Ability Level: Grades 1–4

Teaching Suggestions

The test is a curriculum tool. Follow the pattern test-teach. Teaching the instant words should be only a part of your reading instruction program.

1. Flashcards: Any word the student does not "instantly" read correctly, set aside for repetition later in the lesson and the next day.

2. Easy Reading: Instant words are encountered in all reading, so encouraging frequent independent reading will increase fluency and word recognition. (independent level on the Oral Reading Test)

3. Games: Many word games can be created using the instant words. These games are fun and motivating for students to play. Suggested ideas: Bingo, Pairs, or make a board game.

4. Spelling: Use the instant words for spelling lessons.

Instant Word Comprehensive Test

Directions: Have the student read the words aloud from the student's copy on page 31. On this page, mark **C** for each word read correctly and **X** for each word read incorrectly.

Student's Name: _____

Rank Number		Rank Number		Rank Number		Rank Number	
_____1.	the	_____26.	or	_____51.	will	_____76.	number
_____2.	of	_____27.	one	_____52.	up	_____77.	no
_____3.	and	_____28.	had	_____53.	other	_____78.	way
_____4.	a	_____29.	by	_____54.	about	_____79.	could
_____5.	to	_____30.	word	_____55.	out	_____80.	people
_____6.	in	_____31.	but	_____56.	many	_____81.	my
_____7.	is	_____32.	not	_____57.	then	_____82.	than
_____8.	you	_____33.	what	_____58.	them	_____83.	first
_____9.	that	_____34.	all	_____59.	these	_____84.	water
_____10.	it	_____35.	were	_____60.	so	_____85.	been
_____11.	he	_____36.	we	_____61.	some	_____86.	call
_____12.	was	_____37.	when	_____62.	her	_____87.	who
_____13.	for	_____38.	your	_____63.	would	_____88.	oil
_____14.	on	_____39.	can	_____64.	make	_____89.	now
_____15.	are	_____40.	said	_____65.	like	_____90.	find
_____16.	as	_____41.	there	_____66.	him	_____91.	long
_____17.	with	_____42.	use	_____67.	into	_____92.	down
_____18.	his	_____43.	an	_____68.	time	_____93.	day
_____19.	they	_____44.	each	_____69.	has	_____94.	did
_____20.	I	_____45.	which	_____70.	look	_____95.	get
_____21.	at	_____46.	she	_____71.	two	_____96.	come
_____22.	be	_____47.	do	_____72.	more	_____97.	made
_____23.	this	_____48.	how	_____73.	write	_____98.	may
_____24.	have	_____49.	their	_____74.	go	_____99.	part
_____25.	from	_____50.	if	_____75.	see	_____100.	over

28

Instant Word Comprehensive
Test *(cont.)*

Directions: Have the student read the words aloud from the student's copy on page 32. On this page, mark **C** for each word read correctly and **X** for each word read incorrectly.

Student's Name: _____

Rank Number		Rank Number		Rank Number		Rank Number	
_____101.	new	_____126.	great	_____151.	put	_____176.	kind
_____102.	sound	_____127.	where	_____152.	end	_____177.	hand
_____103.	take	_____128.	help	_____153.	does	_____178.	picture
_____104.	only	_____129.	through	_____154.	another	_____179.	again
_____105.	little	_____130.	much	_____155.	well	_____180.	change
_____106.	work	_____131.	before	_____156.	large	_____181.	off
_____107.	know	_____132.	line	_____157.	must	_____182.	play
_____108.	place	_____133.	right	_____158.	big	_____183.	spell
_____109.	year	_____134.	too	_____159.	even	_____184.	air
_____110.	live	_____135.	mean	_____160.	such	_____185.	away
_____111.	me	_____136.	old	_____161.	because	_____186.	animal
_____112.	back	_____137.	any	_____162.	turn	_____187.	house
_____113.	give	_____138.	same	_____163.	here	_____188.	point
_____114.	most	_____139.	tell	_____164.	why	_____189.	page
_____115.	very	_____140.	boy	_____165.	ask	_____190.	letter
_____116.	after	_____141.	follow	_____166.	went	_____191.	mother
_____117.	thing	_____142.	came	_____167.	men	_____192.	answer
_____118.	our	_____143.	want	_____168.	read	_____193.	found
_____119.	just	_____144.	show	_____169.	need	_____194.	study
_____120.	name	_____145.	also	_____170.	land	_____195.	still
_____121.	good	_____146.	around	_____171.	different	_____196.	learn
_____122.	sentence	_____147.	form	_____172.	home	_____197.	should
_____123.	man	_____148.	three	_____173.	us	_____198.	America
_____124.	think	_____149.	small	_____174.	move	_____199.	world
_____125.	say	_____150.	set	_____175.	try	_____200.	high

Instant Word Comprehensive Test *(cont.)*

Directions: Have the student read the words aloud from the student's copy on page 33. On this page, mark **C** for each word read correctly and **X** for each word read incorrectly.

Student's Name: _____

Rank Number		Rank Number		Rank Number		Rank Number	
____201.	every	____226.	left	____251.	until	____276.	idea
____202.	near	____227.	don't	____252.	children	____277.	enough
____203.	add	____228.	few	____253.	side	____278.	eat
____204.	food	____229.	while	____254.	feet	____279.	face
____205.	between	____230.	along	____255.	car	____280.	watch
____206.	own	____231.	might	____256.	mile	____281.	far
____207.	below	____232.	close	____257.	night	____282.	Indian
____208.	country	____233.	something	____258.	walk	____283.	real
____209.	plant	____234.	seem	____259.	white	____284.	almost
____210.	last	____235.	next	____260.	sea	____285.	let
____211.	school	____236.	hard	____261.	began	____286.	above
____212.	father	____237.	open	____262.	grow	____287.	girl
____213.	keep	____238.	example	____263.	took	____288.	sometimes
____214.	tree	____239.	begin	____264.	river	____289.	mountain
____215.	never	____240.	life	____265.	four	____290.	cut
____216.	start	____241.	always	____266.	carry	____291.	young
____217.	city	____242.	those	____267.	state	____292.	talk
____218.	earth	____243.	both	____268.	once	____293.	soon
____219.	eye	____244.	paper	____269.	book	____294.	list
____220.	light	____245.	together	____270.	hear	____295.	song
____221.	thought	____246.	got	____271.	stop	____296.	leave
____222.	head	____247.	group	____272.	without	____297.	family
____223.	under	____248.	often	____273.	second	____298.	body
____224.	story	____249.	run	____274.	late	____299.	music
____225.	saw	____250.	important	____275.	miss	____300.	color

Instant Word Comprehensive Test

Directions: Please read this list of words out loud for your teacher.

1. the	26. or	51. will	76. number
2. of	27. one	52. up	77. no
3. and	28. had	53. other	78. way
4. a	29. by	54. about	79. could
5. to	30. word	55. out	80. people
6. in	31. but	56. many	81. my
7. is	32. not	57. then	82. than
8. you	33. what	58. them	83. first
9. that	34. all	59. these	84. water
10. it	35. were	60. so	85. been
11. he	36. we	61. some	86. call
12. was	37. when	62. her	87. who
13. for	38. your	63. would	88. oil
14. on	39. can	64. make	89. now
15. are	40. said	65. like	90. find
16. as	41. there	66. him	91. long
17. with	42. use	67. into	92. down
18. his	43. an	68. time	93. day
19. they	44. each	69. has	94. did
20. I	45. which	70. look	95. get
21. at	46. she	71. two	96. come
22. be	47. do	72. more	97. made
23. this	48. how	73. write	98. may
24. have	49. their	74. go	99. part
25. from	50. if	75. see	100. over

Instant Word Comprehensive
Test *(cont.)*

Directions: Please read this list of words out loud for your teacher.

101. new	126. great	151. put	176. kind
102. sound	127. where	152. end	177. hand
103. take	128. help	153. does	178. picture
104. only	129. through	154. another	179. again
105. little	130. much	155. well	180. change
106. work	131. before	156. large	181. off
107. know	132. line	157. must	182. play
108. place	133. right	158. big	183. spell
109. year	134. too	159. even	184. air
110. live	135. mean	160. such	185. away
111. me	136. old	161. because	186. animal
112. back	137. any	162. turn	187. house
113. give	138. same	163. here	188. point
114. most	139. tell	164. why	189. page
115. very	140. boy	165. ask	190. letter
116. after	141. follow	166. went	191. mother
117. thing	142. came	167. men	192. answer
118. our	143. want	168. read	193. found
119. just	144. show	169. need	194. study
120. name	145. also	170. land	195. still
121. good	146. around	171. different	196. learn
122. sentence	147. form	172. home	197. should
123. man	148. three	173. us	198. America
124. think	149. small	174. move	199. world
125. say	150. set	175. try	200. high

Instant Word Comprehensive
Test *(cont.)*

Directions: Please read this list of words out loud for your teacher.

201. every	226. left	251. until	276. idea
202. near	227. don't	252. children	277. enough
203. add	228. few	253. side	278. eat
204. food	229. while	254. feet	279. face
205. between	230. along	255. car	280. watch
206. own	231. might	256. mile	281. far
207. below	232. close	257. night	282. Indian
208. country	233. something	258. walk	283. real
209. plant	234. seem	259. white	284. almost
210. last	235. next	260. sea	285. let
211. school	236. hard	261. began	286. above
212. father	237. open	262. grow	287. girl
213. keep	238. example	263. took	288. sometimes
214. tree	239. begin	264. river	289. mountain
215. never	240. life	265. four	290. cut
216. start	241. always	266. carry	291. young
217. city	242. those	267. state	292. talk
218. earth	243. both	268. once	293. soon
219. eye	244. paper	269. book	294. list
220. light	245. together	270. hear	295. song
221. thought	246. got	271. stop	296. leave
222. head	247. group	272. without	297. family
223. under	248. often	273. second	298. body
224. story	249. run	274. late	299. music
225. saw	250. important	275. miss	300. color

Letter Names Test

Purpose

Knowing the names of all the letters in the alphabet is a useful skill. Success in doing this has been found to be highly correlated with success in beginning reading.

Suggested Reading Ability Level: Grades K–1

Some educators recommend teaching capital letters at kindergarten or pre-school level. Students should know both capitals and lower case letters by mid-first grade.

Teaching Suggestions

1. Oral Practice: Ask a student to point to a known letter in a story, advertisement, or any print. Point to other letters and ask the student to name each letter. Practice with the letters that the student misses. Observe whether they are capital letters or lower case letters to see with which letters the student is having difficulty.

2. Writing: Learning to write letters is a good way to learn letter names. Use a handwriting chart for stroke order.

3. Dictation Practice: Dictate an alphabet letter. The student writes it. Specify upper or lower case.

4. Flashcards: Flash the letter; the student says the letter name.

5. Alphabet Books: Books with pictures along with letters are especially helpful with younger children.

Name _____

Letter Names Test

Directions: Read each letter out loud for your teacher.

Let's practice in this box.							
m	r	E	j	R	d	v	Q

Test Letters

1.	a	G	i	p	W	s
2.	h	K	u	O	m	X
3.	Y	t	Z	P	A	e
4.	b	H	c	N	D	f
5.	B	I	M	C	F	L
6.	T	g	J	n	k	w
7.	q	v	d	E	M	T

All correct (check here) _____

Letters missed _____

Fluency (speed in naming)

very slow _____   slow _____   average _____   fairly rapid _____   rapid _____

Picture Nouns Test

Purpose

To determine the student's ability to read picture nouns.

Answer Key

1. boy		11. six
2. ball		12. grapes
3. one		13. flower
4. shirt		14. moon
5. cat		15. lake
6. table		16. horse
7. cup		17. cook
8. car		18. radio
9. bread		19. pen
10. water		20. book

Suggested Reading Ability Level: Grades 2–5

Teaching Suggestions

1. Flashcards: Make your own with the word on one side and the picture on the other side or buy them ready-made.

   a. (The teacher flashes a word; the student says it.)

   b. The student silent reads for self-teaching practice or a self test. The student gets a small stack of cards, tries to read the word side, then turns card over to see the picture to check if she or he is correct. The student puts each card into a known pile or an unknown pile. The teacher checks the known pile and teaches from the unknown pile.

2. All of the words in every item on the test can be used for reading instruction, the classroom word wall, or games.

3. All of the words can be used for spelling instruction. See suggestions for spelling instruction on page 53.

4. The picture nouns should be taught along with instant words; limit the number taught in each lesson.

Name _____

Picture Nouns Test

Directions: Circle or point to the word which best describes the picture.

1. boy	girl	baby	woman	man
2. train	game	doll	ball	toy
3. one	two	three	four	five
4. dress	pants	shirt	hat	shoes
5. rabbit	cat	fish	dog	bird
6. table	chair	sofa	chest	desk
7. spoon	fork	bowl	plate	cup
8. boat	truck	car	plane	bus
9. soup	apple	cereal	bread	meat
10. malt	soda	juice	milk	water

Name _____

Picture Nouns Test *(cont.)*

Directions: Circle or point to the word which best describes the picture.

11.	seven	eight	six	ten	nine
12.	orange	fruit	grapes	banana	pear
13.	bush	flower	grass	plant	tree
14.	rain	cloud	star	moon	sun
15.	lake	hill	field	dirt	rock
16.	pig	chicken	duck	horse	cow
17.	nurse	policeman	doctor	farmer	cook
18.	movie	television	radio	ballgame	band
19.	pencil	pen	crayon	chalk	computer
20.	newspaper	magazine	sign	book	letter

Picture Nouns Test (cont.)

Pictures 1–6

Picture Nouns Test *(cont.)*

Pictures 7–12

7.

10.

8.

11.

9.

12.

Picture Nouns Test *(cont.)*

Pictures 13–20

13.

14.

15.

16.

17.

18.

19.

20.

Silent Reading Comprehension Tests

Purpose

These two Silent Reading Comprehension Tests are designed to give you a general idea of a student's comprehension ability in a short period of time. They are shorter than most regular comprehension tests, and therefore not quite as precise. However, they are a good supplement to classroom observation, and will help you find out if further assessment is needed in this area.

Administration and Scoring

Make the appropriate number of copies needed for the group taking this test. Read the directions below with the students and then tell them to begin.

Read the stories and questions about the stories. You are to read each story carefully and then check the box next to the best answer to the question. You may look back at a story if it helps you answer the question. Don't rush, but don't waste time either.

You can tell how each student compares with typical third graders on Test A and with typical seventh graders on Test B. It doesn't make any difference what age or grade each student happens to be. The test items and scoring are from an earlier copy of the National Assessment of Educational Progress (NAEP).

The Answer Key tells you the type of comprehension tested (vocabulary, main idea, inference, and so on) for each item, as well as the percentage of students passing the item at grade level three or seven. This gives you an idea of the item difficulty and the kinds of abilities in which your student may be strong or weak.

A total score (total number of items correct) also gives a more general notion of your student's reading comprehension abilities. A total score of eight correct on Test A would be average for nine-year-olds, who would most likely be in mid-third grade. A total score of seven correct on Test B would be average for thirteen-year-olds, who would most likely be in mid-seventh grade. You can see how your students do in comparison with these guidelines.

Suggested Reading Ability Levels: Test A — Grades 1–4; Test B — Grades 5–8

Teaching Suggestions

Everything you do to teach reading will help students improve in silent reading comprehension. But here are a few specific suggestions:

1. Encourage lots of easy reading at the student's independent reading level in a wide variety of types and subjects: books, magazines, directions, etc.
2. Provide comprehension instruction by asking questions ranging from literal level to critical level. Some question types that will help you can be seen in the next test of oral comprehension questions.
3. Explain all or part of the story or article graphically by drawing an illustration, story graph, time line, outline, or map.
4. Teach and discuss vocabulary. See teaching suggestions for Word Meaning Test.

Silent Reading Comprehension Tests (cont.)

Answer Key for Test A (pages 44–46):

Test A is intended for nine-year-olds, third grade. A score of eight correct is average for nine-year-olds, who would most likely be in mid-third grade. It indicates average third grade reading ability.

Item	Answer	Question Type	Percent of Success for Nine-Year-Olds (National Norms)
1	b	Vocabulary	92%
2	d	Reference	63%
3	d	Facts	86%
4	d	Organization	83%
5	e	Main Idea	84%
6	c	Inferences	75%
7	b	Inferences	86%
8	c	Inferences	60%
9	c	Critical Reading	75%
10	a	Critical Reading	75%

Answer Key for Test B (pages 47–50):

Test B is intended for thirteen-year-olds, seventh grade. A score of seven correct is average for thirteen-year-olds, who would most likely be in mid-seventh grade. It indicates average seventh grade reading ability.

Item	Answer	Question Type	Percent of Success for Thirteen-Year-Olds (National Norms)
1	b	Vocabulary	76%
2	c	Reference	74%
3	a	Facts	68%
4	d	Organization	90%
5	c	Main Idea	88%
6	b	Inferences	86%
7	e	Inferences	72%
8	e	Inferences	55%
9	b	Critical Reading	56%
10	b	Critical Reading	50%

Name _____

Silent Reading Comprehension
Test A

Directions: Read the stories and questions about the stories. You are to read each story carefully and then check the box next to the best answer to the question. You may look back at a story if it helps you answer the question. Don't rush, but don't waste time either.

1. **Read the statements and do what they tell you to do.**

   ☐ a. If you have ever visited the moon, fill in the box here.

   ☐ b. If you have never visited the moon, fill in the box here.

2. **You want to call Mr. Jones on the telephone. You look in the telephone book for his number. You would find it between which names?**

   ☐ a. Jackson and Jacobs   ☐ d. Johnson and Judson

   ☐ b. Jacobs and James   ☐ e. Judson and Justus

   ☐ c. James and Johnson   ☐ f. I don't know.

3. **Read the story and complete the sentence that follows it.**

   The wind pushed the boat farther and farther out to sea. It started to rain, and the fog grew thick. The boy and his father were lost at sea.

   The weather was

   ☐ a. calm.   ☐ d. wet.

   ☐ b. dry.   ☐ e. I don't know.

   ☐ c. sunny.

4. **Read the story and answer the question which follows it.**

   The wind pushed the boat farther and farther out to sea. It started to rain, and the fog grew thick. The boy and his father were lost at sea. What happened first in the story?

   ☐ a. It became foggy.   ☐ d. The boat went out to sea.

   ☐ b. It started to rain.   ☐ e. I don't know.

   ☐ c. The boat turned over.

Name _____

Silent Reading Comprehension
Test A *(cont.)*

5. Read the passage and answer the question which follows it.

A sports car differs from an ordinary passenger car in that its size and number of accessories are limited. The sports car also differs from the ordinary passenger car in performance. It can attain higher speeds because it is built smaller and lower. For these reasons, it can also turn corners faster and more smoothly than a passenger car. Also, a sports car generally gets better gas mileage than an ordinary passenger car.

What does the writer tell you about sports cars?

☐ a. Prices

☐ b. Colors and styles

☐ c. Places to buy them

☐ d. Number of people they hold

☐ e. How sports cars differ from passenger cars

☐ f. I don't know.

6. This is a game to see if you can tell what the nonsense word in the paragraph stands for. The nonsense word is just a silly word for something that you know very well. Read the paragraph and see if you can tell what the underlined nonsense word stands for.

Most people have two cags. You use your cags to hold things when you eat or brush your teeth. Some people write with their left cag, and some people write with their right cag.

Cags are probably

☐ a. eyes.

☐ b. feet.

☐ c. hands.

☐ d. pencils.

☐ e. I don't know.

7. Read the story and answer the question that follows it.

The wind pushed the boat farther and farther out to sea. It started to rain, and the fog grew thick. The boy and his father were lost at sea.

At least how many people were in the boat?

☐ a. one

☐ b. two

☐ c. three

☐ d. four

☐ e. five

☐ f. I don't know.

Name _____

Silent Reading Comprehension
Test A *(cont.)*

8. **Read the story and answer the question that follows it.**

Christmas was only a few days away. The wind was strong and cold. The sidewalks were covered with snow. The downtown streets were crowded with people. Their faces were hidden by many packages as they went in one store after another. They all tried to move faster as they looked at the clock.

When did the story probably happen?

☐ a. November 28   ☐ d. December 25

☐ b. December 1   ☐ e. December 28

☐ c. December 21   ☐ f. I don't know.

9. **Read the story about a fish and answer the question that follows it.**

Once there was a fish named Big Eyes who was tired of swimming. He wanted to get out of the water and walk like other animals do. So one day, without telling anyone, he just jumped out of the water, put on his shoes, and took a long walk around the park.

What do you think the person who wrote this story was trying to do?

☐ a. tell you what fish are like   ☐ d. tell you that fish don't like to swim

☐ b. tell you that fish wear shoes   ☐ e. I don't know.

☐ c. tell you a funny story about a fish

10. **If you listen carefully to what a person says, you can usually tell a lot about him. Sometimes you can tell how he feels. Read the passage and complete the sentence that follows it.**

"I'll be glad when this TV show is over. I like stories about spies, not this one about cowboys and Indians. I get to pick the next show."

The person who said this

☐ a. likes spy stories.

☐ b. doesn't like TV at all.

☐ c. doesn't care what TV show is on.

☐ d. likes stories about cowboys and Indians.

☐ e. I don't know.

Name _____

Silent Reading Comprehension Test B

Directions: Below are a number of stories and questions about the stories. You are to read each story carefully and then check the box next to the best answer to the question. You may look back at a story if it helps you answer the question. Don't rush, but don't waste time either.

1. **Read the sentence and fill in the box beside the group of words which tells what the sentence means.**

   "I certainly won't miss that movie."

   ☐ a. I like that movie.

   ☐ b. I'm going to that movie.

   ☐ c. I'm not going to that movie.

   ☐ d. I hope I'll see that movie, but I don't know if I can.

   ☐ e. I didn't see that movie, although it was here all fall.

   ☐ f. I don't know.

2. **Read the following directions taken from a can of insecticide spray and answer the question which follows them.**

   ABC Bug Spray

   Kills: spiders, roaches, ants, and most other crawling insects

   Directions: Spray surfaces over which insects may crawl: doorways, window ledges, cracks, etc. Hold can approximately 10 inches from surface. Do not use near uncovered food or small children. Toxic.

   Which of the following will probably not be killed by the spray?

   ☐ a. ants ☐ d. roaches

   ☐ b. caterpillars ☐ e. spiders

   ☐ c. flies ☐ f. I don't know.

3. **What is the best way to find out if there is something about Eskimos in a book?**

   ☐ a. Look in the index. ☐ d. Look through all the pages.

   ☐ b. Look in the glossary. ☐ e. Skim through the introduction.

   ☐ c. Look at the title page. ☐ f. I don't know.

Name _____

Silent Reading Comprehension Test B *(cont.)*

4. **Read the passage and answer the question which follows it.**

   It should come as no surprise to learn that 9 out of 10 Americans are in debt. In fact, 5 out of 10 are heavily in debt. The amount of debt is shown in government statistics that reveal income has increased 50% while debts have increased 110%!

   Putting statistics into their proper perspective: We learn paying off the car, the home, the groceries, the doctors, and even the children's education on credit is now a way of life for over a hundred million Americans. Very few of us could get by if we had to pay cash when we buy. Living a comfortable lifestyle is made easier for us by payment plans, easy-to-acquire charge cards, and easy-to-borrow bank loans.

   According to the article, how many Americans are in debt?

   ☐ a. 50%

   ☐ b. 2 out of 3

   ☐ c. 4 out of 5

   ☐ d. 9 out of 10

   ☐ e. I don't know.

5. **Read the two stories and answer the question which follows them.**

   Story 1

   A handsome prince was riding his horse in the woods. He saw a dragon chasing a beautiful princess. The prince killed the dragon. The prince and the princess were then married.

   Story 2

   Mary was taking a boat ride on a lake. The boat tipped over. Mary was about to drown when a young man jumped in the lake and saved her.

   If Story 2 ends like Story 1, what would happen next in Story 2?

   ☐ a. A prince would kill a dragon.

   ☐ b. The young man would become a prince.

   ☐ c. Mary and the young man would get married.

   ☐ d. The kid would give the young man some money.

   ☐ e. I don't know.

Name _____

Silent Reading Comprehension Test B (cont.)

6. Read the story and answer the question which follows it.

Sammy got to school ten minutes after the school bell had rung. He was breathing hard and had a black eye. His face was dirty and scratched. One leg of his pants was torn.

Tommy was late to school, too; however, he was only five minutes late. Like Sammy, he was breathing hard, but he was happy and smiling.

Sammy and Tommy had been fighting. Who probably won?

☐ a. Sammy

☐ b. Tommy

☐ c. I cannot tell from the story.

☐ d. I don't know.

7. Read the passage and answer the question which follows it.

One spring, Farmer Brown had an unusually good field of wheat. Whenever he saw any birds in this field, he got angry and tried to chase them away.

In the middle of the summer he found that the insects had multiplied very fast. What Farmer Brown did not understand was this: A bird is not simply an animal that eats food the farmer may want for himself. Instead, it is one of many links in the complex surroundings, or environment, in which we live.

How much grain a farmer can raise on an acre of ground depends on many factors. Such things as the richness of soil, the amount of rainfall, the amount of sunlight, and the temperature belong together in one group called living factors. The living factors in any plant's environment are animals and other plants. Wheat, for example, may be damaged by wheat rust, a tiny plant that feeds on wheat; or it may be eaten by plant-eating animals such as birds or grasshoppers.

It is easy to see that the relations of plants and animals to their environment are very complex and that any change in the environment is likely to bring about a whole series of changes.

What important idea about nature does the writer want us to understand?

☐ a. Farmer Brown was worried about the heavy rainfall.

☐ b. Nobody needs to have such destructive birds around.

☐ c. Farmer Brown didn't want the temperature to change.

☐ d. All insects need not only wheat rust but grasshoppers.

☐ e. All living things are dependent on other living things.

☐ f. I don't know.

Name _____

Silent Reading Comprehension Test B *(cont.)*

8. Read the passage and complete the sentence that follows it.

Art says that the polar ice cap is melting at the rate of 3% per year. Bert says that this isn't true because the polar ice cap is really melting at the rate of 7% per year.

We know for certain that

☐ a. Art is wrong.

☐ b. Bert is wrong.

☐ c. they are both wrong.

☐ d. they both might be right.

☐ e. they can't both be right.

☐ f. I don't know.

9. Read the passage and answer the question that follows it.

Johnny told Billy that he could make it rain any time he wanted to by stepping on a spider. Billy said he couldn't. Johnny stepped on a spider. That night it rained. The next day Johnny told Billy, "That proves I can make it rain any time I want to."

Was Johnny right?

☐ a. Yes

☐ b. No

☐ c. Can't tell from the passage

☐ d. I don't know.

10. Read the poem and answer the question that follows it.

My body a rounded stone
With a pattern of smooth seams,
My head a short snake,
Retractive, protective.
My legs come out of their sleeves
Or shrink within,
And so does my chin.
My eyelids are quick clamps.
My back is my roof.
I am always at home.
I travel where my house walks.
It is a smooth stone.
It floats within the lake,
Or rests in the dust.
My flesh lives tenderly
Inside its home.

Which word best describes the speaker in the poem?

☐ a. confused

☐ b. content

☐ c. excited

☐ d. restless

☐ e. unhappy

☐ f. I don't know.

Oral Comprehension Questions

Purpose

This is another way to find out about a student's reading comprehension. Using it orally will give you some insights you might not get with a standardized test or even from written answers.

Suggested Reading Ability Level: Grades 1–8

Teaching Suggestions

Each question type can suggest an area that needs teaching. Teach by:

1. Discussion of these and similar questions. Don't do too many in one lesson.

2. Written responses to one or more questions.

3. Ask about different lengths of reading: a phrase, a sentence, a paragraph, a chapter, etc.

4. Use a variety of reading materials: magazine articles, textbooks, novels, newspapers, etc.

Oral Comprehension Questions

Directions: Select some of the questions you like, or ones that best suit the type of book or story or article the students have read. Use them to informally assess comprehension, for discussion groups, or as individual written responses. Two important guidelines are (1) to use a variety of questions and (2) to limit the number of questions that ask directly stated facts.

1. **Opinion:** Do you like this book? Why?

2. **Comparison:** Is this better than a similar story or article?

3. **Sequence:** What happens first? Next? Before the . . . ?

4. **Setting:** Where does the story or action take place? Would it be different in a different location?

5. **Main Idea:** What point is the writer making? What is the book all about? Could there be a better title? What?

6. **Characters:** What is the hero really like? Who is the worst or weakest character?

7. **Genre:** What is the style of this book? (for example, is it a biography?) Is the writing style informal, believable, or difficult?

8. **Newspaper Questions:** Who? What? Why? When? Where? How? What might happen in the future?

9. **Conclusion:** How does the story end? What would be a better ending? Why? Why do you think the author ends it this way?

10. **Summary:** Retell the story (article) in your own words. Briefly tell us what the story is all about.

11. **Vocabulary:** What are some new words you like, and why do you like them? What are some words about which you aren't sure of the meaning?

12. **Climax:** What is the most interesting part? Scariest? Funniest?

Spelling Test

Purpose

The purpose of this group test is to determine the students' spelling ability for placement in a spelling program.

Scoring

"Levels" are approximate achievement for each grade at the end of the year. These levels can also used with *Dr. Fry's Spelling Book.*

Suggested Reading Ability Level: Primary Grades 1–3; Intermediate Grades 4–6

Teaching Suggestions

1. Correct students' writing. Have the students study and keep a list of misspelled words.

2. Have students do word sorts, sorting out words with similar spelling patterns like onsets, rimes, silent letters, vowel sounds, suffixes, etc.

3. Conduct regular spelling lessons every week all year long. Here is a suggested way of conducting spelling lessons:

- Monday use the Test-Study Method. For example, you might give a spelling test of the 20 words. (Suggested modifications for your grade level: Grades 1 and 2, 10 words, Grades 3 and 4, 15 words, Grades 5 and up, 20 words)

- Have the students correct their own papers.

- Have the students carefully study the words that they missed, paying careful attention to just the incorrect or missing letters, perhaps by circling the incorrect letter(s) and writing the word correctly from memory several times. Have the students play games with their spelling words; for example, play "Bingo," "Fish," or "Pairs" (a matching game) using the spelling words for practice.

- Give a second spelling test on Wednesday.

- Have the students correct their own papers.

- Have the students carefully study the words that they missed, and play more games with the spelling words.

- A final test should be given on Friday only for those students who did not do well on the Wednesday test.

- Each student can keep a chart of his or her scores achieved on the final spelling tests.

Five Step Word Study Method for Students

1. **Look** at the whole word carefully.
2. **Say** the word aloud to yourself.
3. **Spell** each letter to yourself.
4. **Write** the word from memory (cover word and write it).
5. **Check** your written word against the correct spelling (circle errors and repeat Steps 4 and 5).

Spelling Test *(cont.)*

Directions:

1. Give each student a blank sheet of paper.

2. Starting with Number 1, dictate the words:

   a. Say the word.

   b. Use the word in a sentence.

   c. Say the word again (but not more than once).

3. Correct the test yourself, or have students trade papers and correct. (If you have students correct each other's papers, be sure to spot check for accuracy of correction.)

Spelling Test—Primary Levels
Suggested for Grades 1 through 3.

Level 1	Level 2	Level 3	Level 4
1. and	9. small	17. foot	25. fellow
2. girl	10. off	18. break	26. strength
3. which	11. family	19. coat	27. shut
4. can	12. fly	20. loud	28. doubt
5. now	13. heavy	21. bottle	29. tea
6. book	14. over	22. laughed	30. secret
7. these	15. morning	23. service	31. dangerous
8. come	16. difference	24. shook	32. earn

Spelling Test—Intermediate Levels
Suggested for Grades 4 through 6.

Level 3	Level 4	Level 5	Level 6
1. foot	9. fellow	17. film	25. basketball
2. break	10. strength	18. occupied	26. Iowa
3. coat	11. shut	19. gulf	27. anchor
4. loud	12. doubt	20. breeze	28. fuel
5. bottle	13. tea	21. dock	29. February
6. laughed	14. secret	22. store	30. prophet
7. service	15. dangerous	23. paw	31. cane
8. shook	16. earn	24. costume	32. division

Homophones Test A

Purpose

This test determines a student's knowledge of homophones. This includes knowledge of word meaning and spelling.

Answer Key for pages 56–57

1. ant	12. oar	23. Hi	34. close
2. all ready	13. one	24. hole	35. whether
3. eight	14. there	25. Mary	36. lead
4. eye	15. made	26. see	37. principal
5. bear	16. fined	27. pear	38. read
6. ball	17. write	28. read	39. sale
7. sell	18. No	29. peace	40. sent
8. two	19. sum	30. plain	41. so
9. be	20. wood	31. son	42. steal
10. you're	21. hours	32. new	
11. four	22. bye	33. here	

Suggested Reading Ability Level: Grades 3–6

Teaching Suggestions

1. Make additional drill items similar to the tests in this book or buy workbooks containing drills.

2. Make flashcards with a homophone on one side and its matching homophone on the other.

   a. The student reads one side and gives the homophone meaning.

   b. Student reads one side and gives the spelling and meaning of the word on the other side.

3. All of the words in every item on the test can be used for reading instruction, word walls, or games.

4. All of the words can be used for spelling instruction. See suggestions for spelling instruction on page 53.

Name _____

Homophones Test A

Directions: Circle or point to the correct word in parentheses.

1. There is an (ant – aunt) in the sugar bowl.

2. The group was (already – all ready) to go on the trip.

3. If you take away one from nine, you get (eight – ate).

4. Please don't hit me in the (eye – I).

5. The hunter shot a (bear – bare).

6. Don't throw that (ball – bawl) at my head.

7. You can (cell – sell) a lot of ice cream on hot days.

8. John has (to – two) computers.

9. You can (be – bee) friendly with this boy.

10. I hear (your – you're) going to see a movie.

11. He has (four – for) brothers.

12. The boater had an (oar – or – ore) to steer the canoe.

13. I have (one – won) sister.

14. I see a man over (their – there – they're).

15. Father (maid – made) breakfast this morning.

16. The judge (find – fined) the man twenty dollars.

17. Can you (write – right) me a letter soon?

18. (Know – No), I will not go with you.

19. The (some – sum) of 2 and 3 is 5.

20. The man bought (wood – would) to build a house.

21. Twenty-four (hours – ours) make a day.

Name _____

Homophones Test A *(cont.)*

22. She waved good-(buy – by – bye) to me as she left.

23. "(Hi – High) Jane," said Joe as he came in.

24. I have a (hole – whole) in my stocking.

25. Her mother's name is (marry – Mary – merry).

26. You need eyes to (sea – see).

27. A (pair – pear) is good to eat.

28. I (read – red) that book last year.

29. I am working for world (peace – piece).

30. The meaning of your letter is (plain – plane).

31. My father has only one (son – sun).

32. I have a (knew – new) dress.

33. We live (hear – here).

34. We need to (close – clothes) the window; it is cold.

35. He is not certain (weather – whether) to work or rest.

36. These heavy shoes must be made of (lead – led).

37. Our (principal – principle) visits our classroom every day.

38. I like to (read – reed) books.

39. That car is for (sail – sale).

40. Mother (cent – sent) me to the store for milk.

41. Do not walk (sew – so – sow) fast!

42. Robbers (steal – steel) money and other things.

Homophones Test B

Purpose

This test determines a student's knowledge of homophones. (This includes knowledge of word meanings and spellings.)

Answer Key for pages 59–60

1. tails	12. lone	23. wear	34. shown
2. in	13. rowed	24. flower	35. might
3. toe	14. we	25. reigns	36. seam
4. week	15. it's	26. horse	37. sighed
5. blue	16. weigh	27. morn	38. feat
6. brakes	17. meat	28. vary	39. knight
7. creek	18. bin	29. great	40. missed
8. dear	19. shoe	30. through	41. reel
9. die	20. heard	31. need	42. owe
10. fair	21. would	32. heir	
11. beat	22. told	33. add	

Suggested Reading Ability Level: Grades 4–7

Name _____

Homophones Test B

Directions: Circle or point to the correct word in parentheses.

1. Rabbits have very short (tails – tales).

2. Please come (in – inn) the house.

3. I have a hole in the (toe – tow) of my sock.

4. We go to school five days out of the (weak – week).

5. He was wearing (blew – blue) pants.

6. The man will use the (brakes – breaks) to stop the train.

7. That (creak – creek) runs into a nearby river.

8. His brother was very (dear – deer) to him.

9. Did the flowers (die –dye) from cold last night?

10. Our teacher is very (fair – fare).

11. The bad man (beat – beet) his horse.

12. The (loan – lone) traveler was glad to reach home.

13. We (road – rowed) our boat across the lake.

14. Last night (we – wee) went to sleep late.

15. I think (it's – its) going to rain.

16. How much do you think you (way – weigh)?

17. Do you like to eat (meat – meet)?

18. The fruit is in the (bin – been).

19. Mary put her (shoe – shoo) on her left foot.

20. Have you (herd – heard) the bell ring yet?

21. (Wood – Would) you stop playing with your food at the table?

Name _____

Homophones Test B *(cont.)*

22. We were (told – tolled) to wait here.

23. What will you (wear – where) to school today?

24. That (flower – flour) is a beautiful daisy.

25. A king (rains – reigns – reins) over his country.

26. The farmer rode a gray (horse – hoarse).

27. I heard the birds sing early this (morn – mourn).

28. Stars (very – vary) in how bright they are.

29. We are having a (great – grate) birthday party.

30. She read the book all the way (threw – through).

31. I (need – knead) some money to go to the show.

32. The king made his son the (air – heir) to the throne.

33. What two numbers (ad – add) up to three?

34. We were (shown – shone) many cars.

35. He (might – mite) have done it already.

36. There is a hole in the (seam – seem) of my pants.

37. She (side – sighed) with happiness.

38. The man saved the horse, a real (feet – feat).

39. The (knight – night) saved the lady from death.

40. I (missed – mist) getting a ride to school.

41. I have a new (real – reel) for fishing.

42. I know I (oh – owe) you ten dollars.

Word Meaning Test

Purpose

This test determines word meanings through the silent reading of words.

This Word Meaning Test is different from the Instant Word Tests because it tests a student's knowledge of word meanings as well as a student's ability to read the words silently. It is similar to the vocabulary section of many standardized tests.

Administration and Scoring

The directions for the student are at the top of the student test page.

Advise the student not to guess if he or she doesn't know the answer. Scoring stops after the student has made three errors.

Use the answer key on page 62 to score the test. Stop scoring after the student has made three errors. Count the number up to that point. Additional correct answers after the student has made three errors must not be considered in making the total score.

Do not tell the student which answers were correct and which were incorrect because you or another teacher may wish to use this test again. This Word Meaning Test is not like the Instant Words Test or the Phonics Tests on which we urge you to teach the students every item missed. There are plenty of good vocabulary-building materials available for teaching that would be better to use.

Word Meaning Test *(cont.)*

Answer Key for pages 63–64

1. b	6. e	11. e	16. a
2. e	7. d	12. d	17. e
3. d	8. e	13. c	18. b
4. c	9. b	14. d	19. e
5. a	10. e	15. c	20. a

(Don't count any correct answers after 3 errors.)

This test is not normed in the formal sense of most standardized tests; however, the test was anchored to standardized tests. The grade-level scores in the table that follows are approximated. The scores are intended to give you some idea of a student's vocabulary development. For a more accurate designation, you may give a standardized vocabulary test.

Grade-Level Scores Based on Number of Words Right

Number of Words Right	4	5	6	7	8	9	10	11
Approximate Grade Level	3.5	3.8	4.0	4.3	4.5	4.8	5.1	5.5

Number of Words Right	12	13	14	15	16	17	18
Approximate Grade Level	6.0	6.5	6.8	7.1	7.5	8.0	8.5

Teaching Suggestions

1. Emphasize new or interesting words in every subject including reading assignments.

2. Encourage the use of new words in student writing.

3. Teach word roots, prefixes, and homophones using workbooks, flashcards, charts, and crossword puzzles.

Name _____

Word Meaning Test

Directions: Read all the possible answers before choosing one. Choose the word that means the same or tells about the word in heavy type. Circle the correct letter. Do not guess. If you don't know a word, skip it. Stop answering when the words get too hard.

1. **Ink** is used to
   a. walk on.
   b. write with.
   c. cut with.
   d. serve with.
   e. stand on.

2. **Eagle:**
   a. family
   b. cup
   c. lake
   d. coat
   e. bird

3. **Stable:**
   a. husband
   b. window
   c. ocean
   d. building
   e. street

4. A **desert** is very
   a. kind.
   b. strong.
   c. dry.
   d. brave.
   e. dark.

5. **Howl:**
   a. roar
   b. design
   c. propose
   d. depart
   e. succeed

6. **Encyclopedia:**
   a. woman
   b. reason
   c. nation
   d. food
   e. book

7. **Advice:**
   a. record
   b. visit
   c. bridge
   d. opinion
   e. minute

8. **Burlap:**
   a. tunnel
   b. medicine
   c. soil
   d. engine
   e. fabric

9. **Tremendous:**
   a. serious
   b. enormous
   c. religious
   d. famous
   e. precious

10. **Approach** means to come
    a. through.
    b. with.
    c. into.
    d. between.
    e. near.

11. **Abandon:**
    a. look over
    b. hold on
    c. lift up
    d. fall down
    e. give up

12. **Minus:**
    a. about
    b. through
    c. across
    d. less
    e. into

Name _____

Word Meaning Test *(cont.)*

13. **Eligible:**

    a. lonesome

    b. careless

    c. qualified

    d. inferior

    e. profound

14. A **ghetto** is a section of a

    a. story.

    b. wall.

    c. church.

    d. city.

    e. garden.

15. **Exclude:**

    a. educate

    b. excite

    c. eliminate

    d. encourage

    e. ensure

16. **Stage:**

    a. step in a process

    b. tear in a net

    c. condition in a treaty

    d. light in a tower

    e. article in a newspaper

17. **Gratify:**

    a. heat

    b. shout

    c. hope

    d. charge

    e. please

18. **Demote:**

    a. invite

    b. reduce

    c. stroke

    d. pause

    e. excuse

19. **Scavenge:**

    a. check certificates

    b. change residence

    c. support legislation

    d. divide inheritance

    e. remove rubbish

20. **Lank:**

    a. slender

    b. grateful

    c. musical

    d. lively

    e. rare

Graph Reading Test

Purpose

This test shows if the student can accurately gain information from a graph, map, or table.

Answer Key for pages 66–70:

Time Line

1. George Washington
2. No
3. John Q. Adams
4. Thomas Jefferson
5. 7 years

Map Reading

1. a. North
2. d. West
3. c. Lafayette
4. d. 64
5. a. East Fork River
6. c. Bloomington and Columbus
7. a. 30 miles

Bar Graph

1. paper and cardboard
2. rubber and leather
3. 20%
4. 18%
5. glass

Table Reading

1. Hannah Hoes
2. 1842
3. 5 children
4. W. H. Harrison
5. Kentucky
6. 1744

Suggested Reading Ability Level: Grades 4–7

Teaching Suggestions

1. Get a map of your town and your state. Ask questions about location, distance, and direction.

2. Find examples of bar graphs and pie charts in math books, social studies books, newspapers, etc., for discussion.

3. Have students collect graphs and charts for "Show and Tell."

4. Show how a table can condense much information. Generate verbal sentences from a graph.

Name _____

Graph Reading Test

Directions: Study the time line below and answer the questions.

Reading a Time Line

U.S. Presidents' Years of First Elections					
George Washington	John Adams	Thomas Jefferson	James Madison	James Monroe	John Q. Adams
1789	1797	1804	1808	1816	1824

1. Who was the first president?

    _____

2. Was James Monroe president before James Madison?

    _____

3. Who came after James Monroe?

    _____

4. Who was elected in 1804?

    _____

5. How many years passed between John Adams's election and Thomas Jefferson's election?

    _____

Name _____

Graph Reading Test *(cont.)*

Directions: Use the map on page 68 to answer the questions.

Map Reading

1. What direction is Fort Wayne from Indianapolis?
   a. North   b. South   c. East   d. West

2. What direction is Terre Haute from Richmond?
   a. North   b. South   c. East   d. West

3. What town lies between Gary and Indianapolis?
   a. Columbus
   b. Terre Haute
   c. Lafayette
   d. Anderson

4. What highway goes between New Albany and Evansville?
   a. 65   b. 74   c. 69   d. 64

5. The White River runs into which river or lake?
   a. East Fork River
   b. Lake Michigan
   c. Wabash River
   d. Mississinewa Lake

6. Which two cities are closest together?
   a. South Bend and Gary
   b. Indianapolis and Lafayette
   c. Bloomington and Columbus
   d. Muncie and Richmond

7. About how many miles is it from Anderson to Indianapolis?
   a. 30
   b. 60
   c. 90
   d. 120

Name _____

Graph Reading Test *(cont.)*

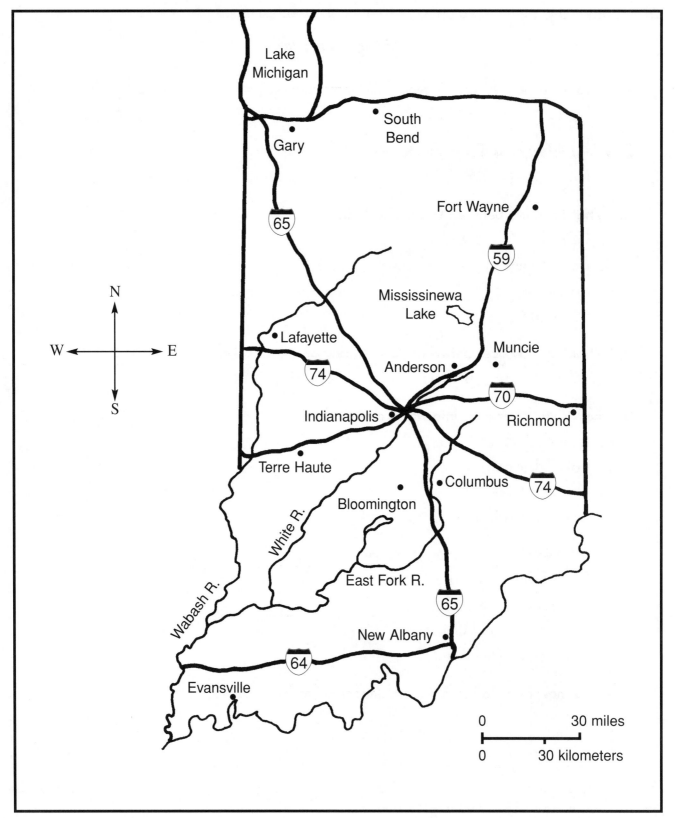

Name _____

Graph Reading Test *(cont.)*

Directions: Use the graph below to answer the questions.

Bar Graph

1. Most of your trash is composed of _____.

2. The smallest amount of your trash is composed of _____.

3. What percent of your trash is yard waste? _____

4. Food waste and metals together make up what percent of your trash? _____

5. Which is more, plastic or glass? _____

What's in Your Trash?

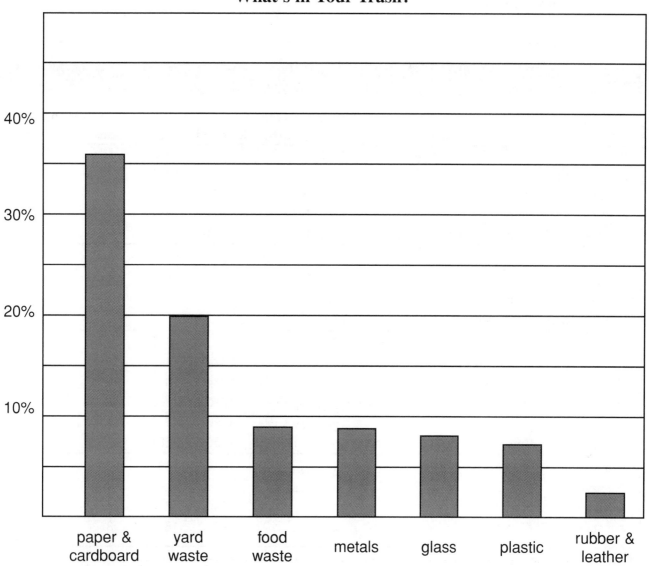

Name _____

Graph Reading Test *(cont.)*

Directions: Use the graph below to answer the questions.

Reading a Table

1. Who was President Van Buren's wife? _____

2. When did President Tyler's first wife die? _____

3. How many children did President John Adams have? _____

4. Which president had the most sons? _____

5 Where was President Lincoln's wife born? _____

6. What year was Abigail Smith born? _____

Wives and Children of the Presidents

President	Wife's name	Year and place of wife's birth	Married	Wife died	Children Sons	Daughters
Washington	Martha Dandridge Custis	1732, VA	1759	1802	—	—
John Adams	Abigail Smith	1744, MA	1764	1818	3	2
Jefferson	Martha Wayles Skelton	1748, VA	1772	1782	1	5
Madison	Dorothy "Dolley" Payne Todd	1768, NC	1794	1849	—	—
Monroe	Elizabeth "Eliza" Kortright	1768, NY	1786	1830	—	2
J.Q. Adams	Louisa Catherine Johnson	1775, England	1797	1852	3	1
Jackson	Mrs. Rachel Donelson Robards	1767, VA	1791	1828	—	—
Van Buren	Hannah Hoes	1788, NY	1807	1819	4	—
W.H. Harrison	Anna Symmes	1775, NJ	1795	1864	6	4
Tyler	Letita Christian	1790, VA	1813	1842	3	4
	Julia Gardiner	1820, NY	1844	1889	5	2
Polk	Sarah Childress	1803, TN	1824	1891	—	—
Taylor	Margaret Smith	1788, MD	1810	1852	1	5
Fillmore	Abigail Powers	1798, NY	1826	1853	1	1
	Caroline Carmichael McIntosh	1813, NJ	1858	1881	—	—
Pierce	Jane Means Appleton	1806, NH	1834	1863	3	—
Buchanan	(Unmarried)	—	—	—	—	—
Lincoln	Mary Todd	1818, KY	1842	1882	4	—
A. Johnson	Eliza McCardle	1810, TN	1827	1876	3	2

Hearing Test

Purpose

The purpose is to test hearing with a whisper test.

How to Administer

Have the student face away from you. Very softly whisper these numbers.

1, 24, 57, 12, 98

Ask the student to repeat each number after you whisper it. If the student fails to repeat any number, try the same test on two other students to see if anyone can hear your soft whisper. If the other students hear your whisper, you should retest the first student.

If the first student still fails to repeat any number, you should refer the student for an audiometer test or to a doctor. If reasonable evidence exists to indicate the possibility of hearing difficulty, the student's parent or guardian should be promptly informed.

Use the test sheet to record the student's performance on the whisper test as passing (no mistakes) or failing. The record sheet also allows you to enter the results of any other hearing test and to record your informal observations.

Comments on Use

Some experts believe that hearing problems cause more reading problems than vision problems do. It is also possible that there are plenty of undetected hearing problems in students that cause more general school problems.

The best test for hearing loss is an audiometer test. Many school districts have audiometers or at least make audiometer tests available to their students. If you suspect that a student has a hearing loss, arrange to get an audiometer test done on the student.

Before ordering the audiometer test, try this quick hearing screening test called the Whisper Test.

Hearing loss in children is often temporarily caused by a cold or ear infection; therefore, do not become too alarmed, but inform the parents or guardian so medical advice can be sought.

Hearing Test

Directions: Do not let the student see this form (she or he might read the numbers). Have the student face away from you while you whisper the numbers in the box below. Ask the student to repeat each number. Then check the appropriate spaces for the Whisper Test and for your observations.

Student's Name _____

Numbers for Whisper Test

1	24	57	12	98

Passed _____   Failed _____

Informal Observations

Often asks to have words or phrases repeated? _____

Speech in monotone or too loud? _____ Soreness, pressures or noises in ear? _____
Can't hear things others can? _____

Speech pronunciation poor (may omit S's or TH's)? _____ Turns one ear toward speaker? _____

If student fails on the hearing test or if there are hearing problem symptoms, the student may be referred for a further hearing test.

Referred to _____   Date _____

Other Hearing Test (Possibly an Audiometer Test from School Records)

Test Name _____   Given by _____

Date _____   Result _____

Vision Test

Purpose

The purpose is to test vision at near point and at far point.

How to Administer

The far-point test is conducted by simply asking the students to read letters on the Student Page placed twenty feet away. These letters are the equivalent of a Snellen Chart 20/30 line. The symbol 20/30 means that a person with normal vision could see these letters at thirty feet away but being able to see them at twenty feet is still in the normal range.

To give the far-point test, follow these directions.

1. Place the Student Page twenty feet away in a well-lighted place.

2. Cover one of the student's eyes with a sheet of paper to test each eye separately. (Do not allow the student to just close an eye or to put a hand over it.) Students who wear glasses ordinarily should wear them for this test.

Use the record sheet on page 74 to record the student's performance as passing or failing. Passing means no more than one mistake. Inability to see two or more letters suggests a retest on another day. On the retest, two or more mistakes means failing.

The near-point test is conducted at reading distance, with the student page about sixteen inches away from the eyes. You should follow the same directions as for the far-point test, being sure to cover one of the student's eyes and to have a student who ordinarily wears glasses wear them for the test.

On the near-point test, the student should be able to read all the letters fluently with either eye and with both eyes. If a student makes any mistakes, do a retest on another day. Use the record sheet to record the student's performance as passing (no mistakes) or failing.

If a student also fails a retest for near-point or far-point vision, refer the student to the school nurse or suggest to the parent or guardian that an examination by a vision specialist (opthomologist or optometrist) should be done.

Since these vision tests are so minimal, it is often best to have the school nurse do a follow-up examination before you contact the parent or guardian. However, if reasonable evidence exists to indicate the possibility of vision difficulty, the student's parent or guardian should be notified.

The record sheet includes a place for you to record the results of another eye examination, possibly one given by the school nurse or by a specialist. It also lists symptoms of eye trouble. You can check for these symptoms by observation or by asking the student.

Vision Test

Directions: Do not let the student see this sheet. See Instructions on page 73 for how to administer. Check the appropriate spaces for tests and observations.

Student's Name _____

Far-Point Vision

E	D	F	C	Z	P

Right Eye: Passed _____ Failed _____

Left Eye: Passed _____ Failed _____

Near-Point Vision

N	S	T	R	F
R	C	L	C	T	B

Right Eye: Passed _____ Failed _____

Left Eye: Passed _____ Failed _____

Informal Observations

Red eyes? ____ Holds book abnormally close? ____ Holds book abnormally far? ____
Eyes cross or wander (occasionally)? ____ Double vision? ____ Eyes hurt or burn? ____
Headaches? ____ Vision distortion after eye use? ____ Can't see from back of room? ____
Can't see fine print? ____ Shuts one eye occasionally? ____ Other symptoms? ____

If the student fails on either test, or if there are vision problem symptoms, the student may be referred for a further vision test.

Referred to _____ Date _____

Other Vision Examination (Possibly from School Records)

Test Name _____ Given by _____

Date _____ Result _____

Vision Test *(cont.)*

Far-Point Vision

(20 feet)

E D F C Z P

Vision Test *(cont.)*

Near-Point Vision

(16 inches)

NSTRF
RCLCTB

Writing Checklist

Purpose

The purpose is to suggest things to look for when correcting a student's writing. Students can also use this checklist for correcting their own writing.

Teaching Suggestions

1. Have each student write something every day. Practicing writing improves writing.

2. Write a variety of things: stories, letters, diaries, newspaper articles, book reports, jokes, poems, etc.

3. Quickly write a rough draft and correct spelling, punctuation, and grammar later.

4. Give plenty of praise for every writing attempt. Encourage the use of new words and novel ideas.

Name _____

Writing Checklist

Content
- ☐ Select an interesting topic.
- ☐ Stick to the topic.
- ☐ Use good sources for information.
- ☐ Organize the information carefully (sequence, logical order, Q/A, main idea/supporting details, thesis statement/arguments, etc.).
- ☐ Check the facts.
- ☐ Consider/use graphs, tables, or charts for data.
- ☐ Consider the readers and select words to catch their interest, to help them understand, to create images in their minds, to help them follow the sequence.
- ☐ Use sufficient detail and descriptions.
- ☐ Compose an interesting conclusion.

Format
- ☐ Choose an appropriate title.
- ☐ Use quotations correctly.
- ☐ Use headings and subheadings.
- ☐ Good labels or titles for graphics.
- ☐ Include a list of resources or a bibliography.
- ☐ Number the pages.
- ☐ Include the author's name, class, and date.

Mechanics
- ☐ Check sentences for completeness and sense.
- ☐ Check for consistent verb tense.
- ☐ Check for consistent point of view.
- ☐ Check for subject-verb agreement.
- ☐ Check for proper use of pronouns.
- ☐ Check for spelling.
- ☐ Check for end marks and other punctuation.
- ☐ Check for capital letters and underlining.
- ☐ Check paragraphing and indentations.
- ☐ Check legibility.
- ☐ Check comma use.
- ☐ Check over for use of personal pronouns (like "I").

Graph for Estimating Readability

Purpose

This is a quick way of estimating the difficulty level of any book or article. Its purpose is to help teachers select books on a level where the student can read successfully (without getting frustrated and stopping) and in selecting stories for instruction. This test is a starting point for estimating text difficulty and the information gained from it should be combined with other factors like text characteristics and student background, experience, and interest.

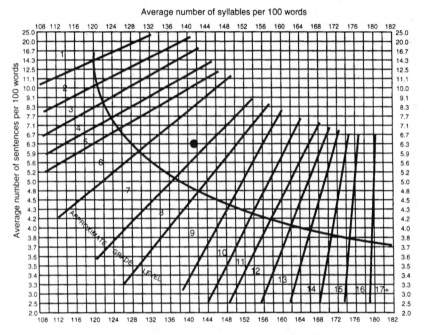

Average number of syllables per 100 words

Directions

Randomly select three passages and count out exactly 100 words each, beginning with the beginning of a sentence. Count the number of sentences in the 100 words, estimating the length of the fraction of the last sentence to the nearest one-tenth. Count the average number of syllables in the 100-word passage. Plot the average number of syllables and average number of sentences per 100 words on the graph to determine the grade level of the material. Choose more passages per book if great variability is observed and conclude that the book has uneven readability. Few books will fall in a gray area, but when they do, grade level scores are invalid. Count proper nouns, numerals, and initializations as words. Count a syllable for each symbol; for example, 1945 is 1 word and 4 syllables and IRA is 1 word and 3 syllables.

Example	Syllables	Sentences
1st Hundred Words	124	6.6
2nd Hundred Words	141	5.5
3rd Hundred Words	158	6.8
Average	141	6.3

Readability = 7th Grade (see plotted dot on graph).

Graph for Estimating Readability

Readability Chart

Title of Book: _____

Publishers: _____ Recommended Level: _____

Date of Publication: _____ Author: _____

Student Friendly?   Yes   Somewhat   No

Content: Excellent   Good   Fair   Poor   Mixed

Passage 1

    page   from   to   # of sentences # of syllables

_____ _____ _____ _____ _____

Passage 2

    page   from   to   # of sentences # of syllables

_____ _____ _____ _____ _____

Passage 3

    page   from   to   # of sentences # of syllables

_____ _____ _____ _____ _____

Comments: _____

_____

_____

_____

_____

Interest Inventory for Children

Directions: To be filled in by the teacher or by the student with teacher assistance; this could be used in selecting interesting stories and reading materials. Most of these items can also be used as story starters or titles for students' themes.

My name is _____.

I am _____ years old.

Outside of school, the thing I like to do best is _____.

In school, the thing I like best is _____.

If I had a million dollars, I would _____.

When I grow up, I will _____.

I don't like _____.

My favorite animal is _____.

The best sport is _____.

When nobody is around, I like to _____.

The person I like best is _____.

Next summer I hope to _____.

My father's work is _____.

My mother's work is _____.

When I grow up, I will be _____.

I like to collect _____.

The things I like to make are _____.

My favorite place to be is _____.

The best book I ever read was _____.

The best TV show is _____.

My favorite school subjects are _____.

Interest Inventory for Adults

Directions: To be filled out by the teacher or by the adult with teacher assistance; this could be used in selecting interesting stories and reading materials. Most of these items can also be used as story starters or titles for students' themes.

My name is _____

Occupation _____ Where _____

Describe briefly what you do. _____

What do you need to read on the job? _____

What do you like to read for pleasure? _____

What is your hobby? _____

What sport are you interested in? _____

What would you do if you won a million dollars?_____

What kind of further schooling might you do?_____

What books have you read? _____

What do you do on vacation? _____

Do you have any hobbies? _____

Have you ever had your eyes and hearing checked? _____

What kind of work would you like to do in the future?_____

If you moved, where would you like to go? _____

What are your favorite kinds of food and drink? _____

Do you have any family problems? _____

What is the best TV show? _____

Parent/Guardian Interview

Purpose

The purpose is to obtain background information through a structured parent/guardian interview.

Comments on Use

Good communication with a student's parent(s) or guardian(s) will often facilitate the teaching of reading. Students, particularly those who are not learning to read well, sometimes have absolutely incredible backgrounds that you can only find out by interviewing the parent or guardian. Sometimes the student never mentions any problems, or mentions them in such an offhand way that they don't seem relevant. Like an interest inventory, a systematic parent or guardian interview can elicit things you might not uncover in a casual conversation.

The Parent/Guardian Interview Form can give some structure to a meeting. You might not want to formally fill out the record sheet in front of the parent or guardian, but looking it over ahead of time will help you to structure the conversation to elicit the desired information. Other teachers may prefer to openly use the record sheet.

The advantage of using the record sheet is it can be put in the student's file to aid a future teacher. Record only objective information gathered from the interview, not rumors or your subjective judgment. Remember, in many instances courts have held that a student's file is open to inspection by the parent or guardian.

The Parent/Guardian Interview Form gives areas of discussion rather than specific questions. The form is intended to be a reminder rather than a mandate.

Parent/Guardian Interview Form

Student's Name _____ Date _____

Class _____

Name of Parent or Guardian Interviewed _____

Relationship _____

Student's Health: Any recent illnesses? Any past serious illnesses? Normal development? Age began walking? Talking? Vision, hearing, or speech difficulties?

_____

_____

_____

_____

Family Makeup: Who is living in the home? Any separations, divorces, or deaths?

_____

_____

_____

_____

Occupations of Parent(s) or Guardian(s): Include part-time work or recent changes.

_____

_____

_____

_____

Parent/Guardian Interview
Form *(cont.)*

Reading Habits: What does the student read at home? How much time is spent in reading? Is a time or place provided for home reading?

_____

_____

_____

_____

Reading Materials: Are there newspapers or magazines in the home? Does the student have a library card? Are there any easy reading books in the home?

_____

_____

_____

_____

Play Habits: What does the student like to do for play or recreation? Kind and number of friends?

_____

_____

_____

_____

Student's Interests: Any hobbies, jobs, or special interests? What would the student like to do but doesn't?

_____

_____

_____

Parent/Guardian Interview
Form *(cont.)*

Future Plans: Are there any plans for moving? Are there any plans for providing special tutoring or private educational supplement?

_____

_____

_____

_____

School Relations: Does the student like school? Does the parent or guardian? Favorite subjects or teachers? History of changing schools?

_____

_____

_____

_____

Always end an interview by asking an open-ended question like, "Is there anything else you would like to tell me?" Parents or guardians sometimes need an opening like this to bring up something that has been bothering them.

_____

_____

_____

_____

Using School Records

Purpose

The purpose of this form is to summarize school records for maximum effectiveness.

School records are sometimes confusing and are not always used properly. School records can give indications of progress. They can also give you realistic expectations, and they can contribute towards a better understanding of the student. There are many types of information you can gather for your School Record Summary.

Age and Grade Placement

Accurate age and grade placement will help you in interpreting other tests and achievement levels. To get the student's age, just ask, "How old are you?" and "When was your last birthday?" If in doubt about the answer, check the school records.

Then obtain an accurate estimate of the student's grade placement. For example, if it is October, the second month of the school year, and the student is in the third grade, then the student's grade placement is three years and two months, or 3.2.

Chronological Age Grade Placement (CAGP)

When you have a student's age and grade placement, you can calculate Chronological Age Grade Placement, or CAGP. This allows you to compare your students' age and grade placement. It is not surprising to find that some students are a year and a half younger than average students in their grade; yet teachers expect them to be reading "up to grade level." Students tend to read more like their age level than their grade placement.

Using School Records *(cont.)*

To calculate CAGP, simply subtract 5.4 from the student's chronological age (CA). The number 5.4 represents five years and four months, the average age at which a child in the United States begins kindergarten. For example, if Johnny is seven years and six months old (7.6), his CAGP is 2.2 (7.6 – 5.4). Thus, we should expect him to read more like a beginning second grader than like a third grader, even if he is currently in the third grade.

However, age is only one way of determining expectation. It is an "in general" or "on the average" way. It is but one factor to be put into a reading diagnosis summary. It is a bit of information not to be lightly discarded but also not to be taken as the whole truth.

Achievement Tests

Group Reading Achievement Tests are the standardized tests given by the district or state. They are useful because of their excellent norming, but they lose in accuracy because they are administered to groups and made so a computer can score them.

To really understand these tests requires more space than we can give here, but you can learn about their strengths and weaknesses in college courses, by reading chapters in reading textbooks, and from test publishers' manuals.

It is important to understand and interpret your students' test scores. The following are suggestions to help:

1. The reading comprehension or paragraph meaning section of the test is probably the most valuable general reading score.

2. Raw scores can be converted into a number of normed scores like grade equivalent scores, percentile scores, or stanines for either United States or local norms.

3. All tests have a certain amount of inaccuracy, which is sometimes given as the standard error of measurement or as a band score.

Using School Records *(cont.)*

Test scores recorded over a period of time, and particularly recent test scores, can help you in your reading diagnosis. Other achievement tests can also contribute towards a better understanding of your student. A spelling score might show a surprising strength, or a good math score might indicate a good bit of potential for improvement.

Remember that the decimal point is usually not printed with IQ scores, so an IQ of 94 is really .94 and an IQ of 115 is really 1.15. The IQ score can be used with a student's chronological age (CA) to calculate a student's mental age (MA). If, for example, Johnny has an IQ of 94 and is 7.6 years old (CA 7.6), then his MA is 7.1. (.94 x 7.6 = 7.144).

Now to convert this to MAGP (mental age grade placement), simply subtract 5.4 as we did with CAGP. Johnny's MAGP is 1.7 (7.1 minus 5.4), so we would expect him to be reading like an upper first grader based on his IQ test.

Thus, MAGP gives you an achievement expectancy based on the IQ score. Here are the calculations in formulas:

$$MAGP = (IQ \times CA) - 5.4$$

And for Johnny in the example above,

$$MAGP = (.94 \times 7.6) - 5.4$$

$$MAGP = 1.7$$

Other Information

School records often contain much other information that might give you some insights into your student's functioning or lack of functioning. Some of the kinds of information you might summarize from the school records or teacher's report are:

- attendance regularity
- teacher changes
- school changes
- health
- problems of behavior
- adjustment

- learning
- strong points in other school subjects
- personality
- extracurricular activity

Using School Records

School Record Summary

Student's Name _____ Date_____

Student's Age _____ years and _____ months _____

Present Grade _____ years and _____ months _____

Chronological Age Grade Placement (CAGP)

This compares the student's age and grade placement with United States norms.

Subtract 5 years and 4 months from the student's age:

CAGP is _____ years, _____ months.

This would be the grade the student would be in if the student started kindergarten at the age of 5 years and 4 months.

Student's CAGP is _____ years and _____ months ahead/behind student's present grade.

Group Reading Achievement Tests

Keep a record of group standardized or other reading tests.

Name of Test	Date	Scores
_____	_____	_____
_____	_____	_____
_____	_____	_____

Other Achievement Tests

Keep a record of achievement tests in other areas such as mathematics, language, social studies, spelling, and science.

Name of Test	Date	Scores
_____	_____	_____
_____	_____	_____
_____	_____	_____

Using School Records *(cont.)*

School Record Summary

Different Schools Attended

Dates   School   City and State

_____   _____   _____

_____   _____   _____

_____   _____   _____

Attendance (Absences)

Grades   Days Absent

_____   _____

_____   _____

_____   _____

Illness—Major illness or physical limitations (not occasional cold)

_____

_____

_____

Problems in Learning or Behavior—Any record of special help, special discipline

_____

_____

_____

Strong Points and Special Interests—Excellent in a subject, extracurricular, talents, interests

_____

_____

_____

Testing Terms

The following is a list of terms that may be helpful to you when trying to interpret various types of assessment tests. Familiarity with these terms can also be of help when explaining test results to students and parents.

Achievement Tests: Tests that measure how much students have learned in a particular subject area.

Aptitude Tests: Tests that attempt to predict how well students will do in learning new subject matter in the future.

Criterion-Referenced Tests: Tests for which the performance of the test taker is compared with a fixed standard or criterion. The primary purpose is to determine if the test taker has mastered a particular unit sufficiently to proceed to the next unit.

Diagnostic Tests: Tests that are used to identify individual student's strengths and weaknesses in a particular subject area.

Grade Equivalent Scores: The grade level for which a score is the real or estimated average. For example, a grade equivalent score of 3.5 is the average score of students halfway through third grade.

Mean: The arithmetical average of a group of scores.

Median: The middle score in a group of scores.

Mode: The score that was obtained by the largest number of test takers.

Normal Distribution: A bell-shaped distribution of test scores in which scores are distributed symmetrically around the mean and where the mean, median, and mode are the same.

Norming Population: The group of people to whom the test was administered in order to establish performance standards for various age or grade levels. When the norming population is composed of students from various sections of the country, the resulting standards are called national norms. When the norming population is drawn from a local school or school district, the standards are referred to as local norms.

Norm-Referenced Tests: Tests for which the results of the test taker are compared with the performance of others (the norming population) who have taken the test.

Percentile Rank: A comparison of an individual's raw score with the raw score of others who took the test (usually this is a comparison with the norming population). This comparison tells the test taker the percentage of other test takers whose scores fell below his or her own score.

Raw Score: The initial score assigned to test performance. This score usually is the number correct; however, sometimes it may include a correction for guessing.

Standard Error of Measurement (SEM): An estimate of the amount of measurement error in a test. This provides an estimate of how much a person's actual test score may vary from his or her hypothetical true score. Some tests give a band score, which is based on SEM. The larger the SEM, the less confidence can be placed in the score as a reflection of a test's true reliability.

Standardized Tests: Tests that have been given to groups of students under standardized conditions and for which norms have been established.

Validity: The extent to which a test measures what it is supposed to measure. Two common types are content validity (the extent to which the content of the test covers situations and subject matter about which conclusions will be drawn) and predictive validity (the extent to which predictions made from the test are confirmed by evidence gathered at some later time).

Normal Distribution Curve

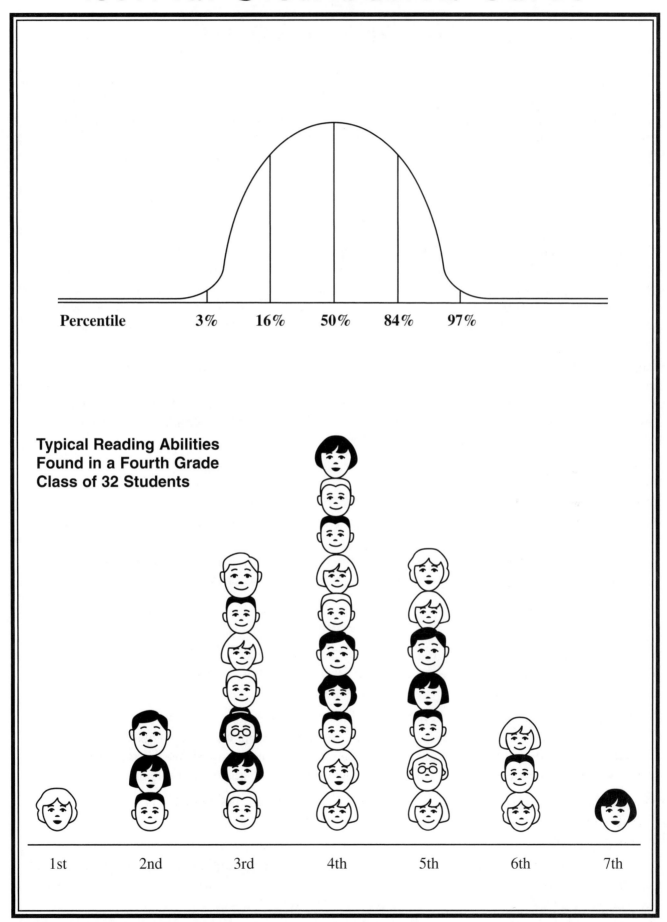

Percentile   3%   16%   50%   84%   97%

Typical Reading Abilities Found in a Fourth Grade Class of 32 Students

1st   2nd   3rd   4th   5th   6th   7th

Tips for Assessment and Recordkeeping

There are many ways to assess the growth and competency of your students. It is important to have a balance of assessment tools and authentic assessment should be part of that balance. The best assessment requires authenticity, relevance, and the involvement of both teacher and student. The tests provided in this book will help to determine your student's progress, to determine areas of difficulty in the area of reading, and to plan instruction. The following strategies will describe a variety of authentic assessment techniques to supplement the tests provided in this book.

Assessment

Observation: When observation is done really well, it allows for immediate intervention. Small groups can be called together for instant mini-lessons on important concepts, partners can be refocused on the task at hand, and an individual student can be guided in the right direction. Recording this type of assessment can be a problem if you do not have a system. Some teachers use anecdotal records, while others use clipboards, checklists, note cards, or sticky notes. Whatever system is used, it is important for it to be recorded with the child's name and the date.

Conferencing: Conferencing is another important part of assessment. Conferences can be formal or informal, planned or spur of the moment. The teacher uses this time to review and to analyze what the student has been doing and to help plan and implement the next steps in the student's learning. The results of the conference should be recorded on a form to be placed in your individual student files. The student can be a part of this recording process.

The Writing Process: The writing process makes up an important part of effective assessment. The multiple drafts that result from this process of self-editing, peer-editing, teacher-editing, revising, and publishing provide a ready-made record of student progress.

Self-Evaluation: Journal entries, reading records, checklists, completed questionnaires, and the students' written reflections on their own work are also useful in tracking students' progress. They are part of the self-evaluation aspect of assessment in which students are asked to rate their own progress and to take ownership of and responsibility for the process as well as the results.

Recordkeeping

Recordkeeping is an essential part of assessment. The records that are kept must represent the range of achievement, the processes that are going on, the effort that is shown, and the improvement that is demonstrated.

Some suggestions for recordkeeping include the following:

- Write down everything you want to remember about a student on a chart, checklist, or other piece of paper that is easy to read and that could be used in a parent conference or student study meeting. The assessment forms from the tests in this book, student work samples, checklists, conferencing notes, and anecdotal records are all good ways to keep records about student growth.

- It is important to record positive statements about progress, as well as noting areas needing improvement.

- Assessment needs to be continuous throughout the year, and your records should reflect this ongoing assessment.

- Date all assessment information.

Research and Classroom Book References

The following is a list of books that you might find helpful to learn more about the teaching and assessment of reading:

Adams, M. J. *Beginning to Read: Thinking and Learning About Print*. Cambridge, MA: The MIT Press. 1990.

Bear, D.R., Invernizzi, M., Templeton, S. and Johnston, F. *Words Their Way: Word Study for Phonics, Vocabulary, and Spelling Instruction*. Columbus, OH: Merrill. 1996.

Burns, P., Roe, B., and Ross, E. *Teaching Reading in Today's Elementary Schools*. Boston: Houghton Mifflin. 1999.

Cramer, R.L. *The Spelling Connection: Integrating Reading, Writing, and Spelling Instruction*. New York: The Guilford Press. 1998.

Cunningham, P.M. *Phonics They Use: Words for Reading and Writing*. New York: HarperCollins. 1995.

Fletcher, J.M. *Research-Based Assessment of Reading and Spelling Skills: Implications for the Classroom*. 1997.

Fountas, I.C., and Pinnell, G.S. *Guided Reading: Good First Teaching for All Children*. Portsmouth, NH: Heinemann. 1996.

Pearson, P.D. "Changing the Face of Reading Comprehension." *The Reading Teacher*, 38(6), 724-738. 1985.

Stanovich, K.E. "Matthew Effects in Reading: Some Consequences of Individual Differences in the Acquisition of Literacy." *Reading Research Quarterly*, 21, 360-407. 1986.

Sulzby, E. "Assessment of writing and of children's language while writing." In L. Morrow & J. Smith (Eds.) *The Role of Assessment and Measurement in Early Literacy Instruction* (pp. 83-109). Englewood Cliffs, N.J.: Prentice-Hall. 1989.

Yopp, H. "Developing Phonemic Awareness in Young Children." *The Reading Teacher,* Vol. 45. 1992.

Teacher Created Materials Reference List:

Bishop, A. and Bishop S. *Teaching Phonics, Phonemic Awareness, and Word Recognition*. TCM 2126. 1996.

Christena, K, and Lynch, M.A. *A Guide To Teaching Beginning Reading For Teachers and Parents*. TCM 2598. 2000.

Flint, A.S. *Literature Circles*. TCM 2480, 1999.

Ryan, C.D. *Authentic Assessment*. TCM 838. 1994.

Ryan, C.D. *Teaching Basic Skills Through Literature*. TCM 839. 1995.

Seely, A. *Portfolio Assessment*. TCM 845. 1994.

Visser, E. and Hanggi, G.M. *Guided Reading in a Balanced Program*. TCM 2477. 1999.

Related Teaching Materials

The following Dr. Fry Teaching Materials may be helpful for you to use after assessing your students. Listed next to each title are the assessment tests that correspond with the teaching materials.

Title and TCM#	Test Number
Student Books:	
Beginning Writer's Manual TCM 2759	12, 14, 18
Homophones (workbook) TCM 2668	12, 13, 14
Instant Word Practice Book (workbook) TCM 3503	6, 7, 12
Picture Nouns TCM 2763	9, 12
Spelling Checker TCM 2669	12, 18
Vocabulary Fun (workbook) TCM 2765	1, 10, 14
Word Book for Beginning Writers TCM 2758	12, 14, 18
Teacher Reference Books:	
How to Teach Reading TCM 2760	1, 2, 3, 4, 5, 6, 7, 8, 9, 10, 11, 14, 15, 18
1000 Instant Words TCM 2757	6, 7, 12
Phonics Patterns TCM 2761	2, 3, 4, 5
Spelling Book (3000 Instant Words) TCM 2750	6, 7, 12
The Reading Teacher's Book of Lists TCM 2648	2, 3, 4, 5, 10, 11, 12, 13, 14, 18
Charts:	
Blends and Digraphs TCM 3504	2, 3
Long Vowels TCM 1769	2, 3, 4, 5
Mixed Vowels TCM 3506	2, 3
Phonics Charts TCM 2762	2, 3, 5
Short Vowels TCM 1796	2, 3, 4, 5
Vowel Combinations TCM 3505	2, 3
Flashcards:	
Alphabet TCM 2666	8
Instant Words Set A TCM 2661	6, 7, 12
Instant Words Set B TCM 2662	6, 7, 12
Phonics Set A TCM 2663	2, 5, 12
Phonics Set B TCM 3502	2, 5, 12
Phonograms TCM 2664	2, 3, 4, 5
Picture Nouns Set A TCM 2665	9, 12
Picture Nouns Set B TCM 3501	9, 12